T0101830

THE YOUNG WITCH'S GUIDE TO CRYSTALS

THE YOUNG WITCH'S GUIDE TO CRYSTALS

CASSANDRA EASON

STERLING CHILDREN'S BOOKS
New York

STERLING CHILDREN'S BOOKS
New York

An Imprint of Sterling Publishing Co., Inc.
1166 Avenue of the Americas
New York, NY 10036

ISBN 978-1-4549-3680-0

Distributed in Canada by Sterling Publishing Co., Inc.
c/o Canadian Manda Group, 664 Annette Street
Toronto, Ontario M6S 2C8, Canada
Distributed in the United Kingdom by GMC Distribution Services
Castle Place, 166 High Street, Lewes, East Sussex BN7 1XU, England
Distributed in Australia by NewSouth Books
University of New South Wales, Sydney, NSW 2052, Australia

For information about custom editions, special sales, and premium and corporate purchases, please contact Sterling Special Sales at 800-805-5489 or specialsales@sterlingpublishing.com.

Manufactured in South Korea

Lot #:
2 4 6 8 10 9 7 5 3 1
05/20

sterlingpublishing.com

Cover and interior design by Irene Vandervoort
Cover illustration by Laura Tolton
Interior illustrations by Eugenia Nobati

To my beloved children Tom, Jade, Jack, Miranda, and Bill.
To my dearest grandchildren Freya, Oliver, Holly, and Sophie.
To John and Konnie Gold.
And a sincere thanks to my editor, Ardi Alspach,
who has opened up a new world of writing for me.

CONTENTS

INTRODUCTION

✳ CRYSTAL MAGIC ✳

Welcome to the school of crystals, young witches. In this book we are going to discover exciting and beautiful additions to your magickal life—crystals! These are often small polished stones of every color and kind. Each has a magickal power and meaning, and they will protect you against negativity of all kinds. You can carry crystals in your purse, in your pocket, or in a tiny bag you hang around your neck or hide inside your clothes. There is a crystal for everything you could possibly imagine, including healing.

You can put crystals around your bed to keep away spooks and bad dreams, or use them as lucky charms and in magick spells. Pick crystals from a bag for telling the future. Collect, hold, and keep crystals because they are beautiful and filled with the power of the earth. They are fairy jewels that can open all kinds of doors to magick and special wishes. You can buy crystal angels, animals, statues, wands, and even crystal skulls that are very protective.

If you are on vacation near the ocean or in a tourist resort, gift stores often sell local stones that will hold memories of your great time there as well as the special power of the place they came from.

You can build your crystal collection through months and years, and you can ask for special crystals for birthdays and holidays. In time, you'll wonder how you ever managed without your crystals.

YOUR CRYSTAL JOURNAL

Keep notes online, on your computer, or in a notebook. Take photos or make illustrations of your crystals and keep notes about them as you get to know them better. You can record the crystal readings you do and keep all information about your zodiac birthstones and any special crystal spells you create. This will be your record of all of your magickal work; it will be a reference you can turn to as your magickal experience grows.

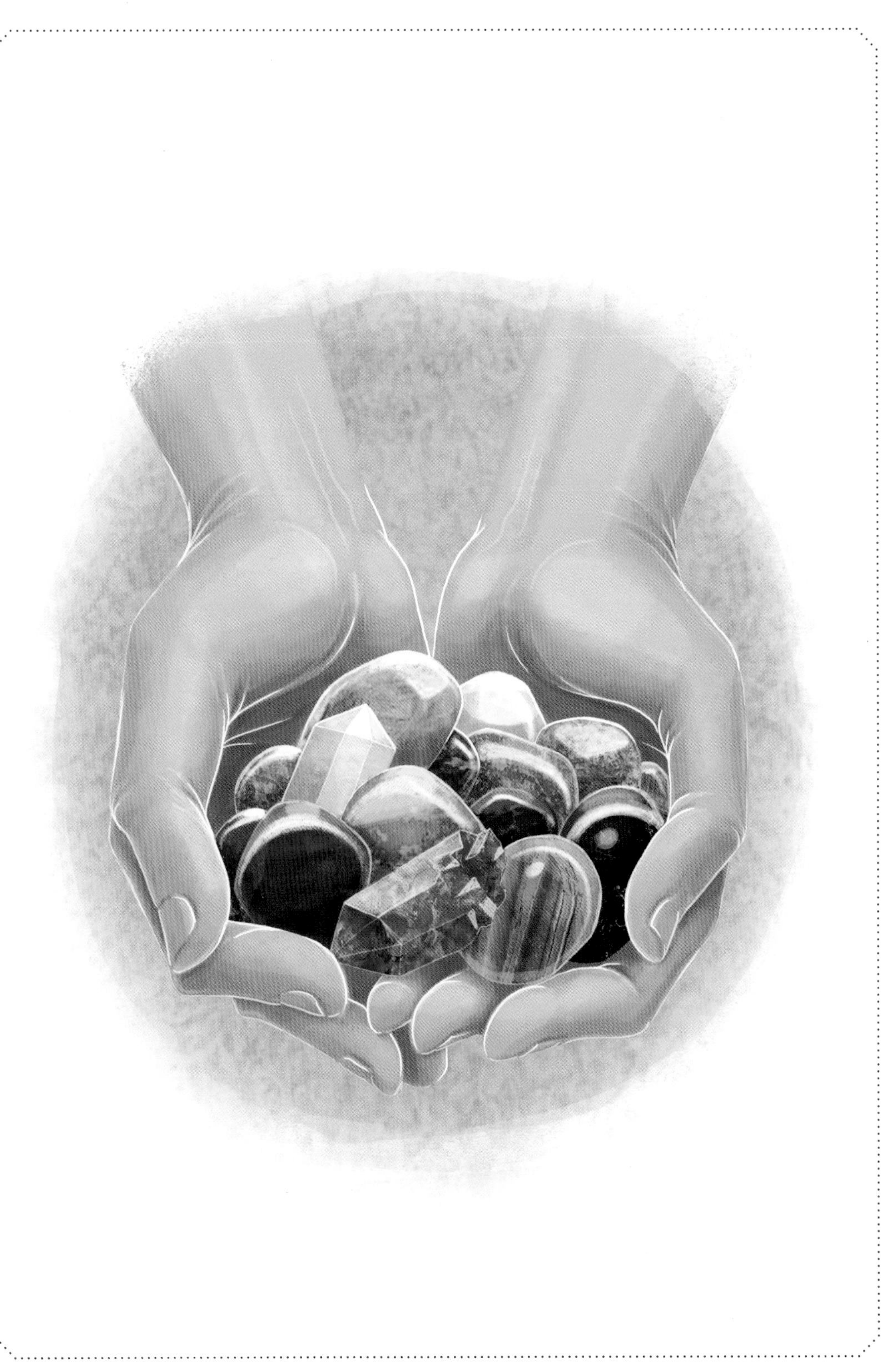

CHAPTER 1

MAKING YOUR CRYSTAL ALTAR

You can use your crystals absolutely anywhere; however, it will become useful to have a special place in your bedroom where you can store and work with your crystals. Use any small table or flat surface in your bedroom as your crystal altar. If you share an apartment, you may be able to team up with friends to create an altar you can use together.

Over time, your altar will become a special space where you can light a candle or some incense, hold your favorite crystal, and allow wishes and dreams to come and go. You don't need all the things listed in this book at first, but a few crystals with a candle and incense will make your altar instantly beautiful—and you can add to it later, because collecting crystals can become a lifetime passion.

YOU WILL NEED:

1. A table or flat surface, covered with a scarf or cloth in your favorite color. You can change this as your mood alters or when you need special powers in your life. You will learn about the magickal meanings of colors in CHAPTERS 4–5.
2. A white candle in the center.
3. Any floral incense stick to the right of the candle and a bowl of water to the left of the candle.
4. In the center in front of the candle, place a small dish to hold the crystals or crystal jewelry you will charge with magickal power. Afterward, you can carry these with you or wear them.
5. Arrange any special crystals you have, such as a crystal angel, animal, or bird. You may also choose a small crystal ball that will give you messages from the spirits. A pendulum, a pointed crystal on a chain, and any larger crystals you collect will come in handy in the future.

YOUR MAGICKAL TREASURE BOX

You will want to keep a box just for your magickal items. In your box, collect candles in different colors, incense in lots of floral fragrances, and small velvet or fabric drawstring bags or purses in different colors. These bags should be a variety of sizes, including tiny ones to carry a single crystal as a charm and ones large enough to contain your fifteen basic crystals described in the next chapter. Over time you can add bowls of small crystals for making crystal layouts. You can pop a few of these colored crystals in a bag to carry their power with you.

You may want a second special box for your crystal jewelry and your birth sign or zodiac stones.

MAKING YOUR CRYSTAL ALTAR MAGICKAL

The first time you use your crystal altar and whenever you add a new crystal, you will want to add power and protection. In the next chapter, you will learn more ways to keep all your crystals powerful and clear of negative energies.

1. Light your candle and incense.
2. Move the palms of your hands a few inches above and all around the outside of your altar (not too near the candle or lighted incense). Let your writing hand make clockwise circles and your other hand counterclockwise circles at the same time for a minute or two.
3. As you do this, say softly and continuously, *"I ask the blessings and protection of the spirits of my crystals. May my crystals always be used to bring happiness and healing to myself and others."*
4. Wave incense smoke all around your altar. Return the incense stick to its holder. Leave the candle and incense to burn.

CRYSTALS AS LUCK BRINGERS

You may already have a lucky crystal ring or pendant of your birthstone (see PAGES 51–52 for a full list). When you wear your lucky birthday charm, things seem to go well, so you feel good and good luck comes your way. But you can fill any crystal with power and good fortune, and that will bring good luck. Every time your crystal attracts good luck, it draws to it extra power like a magnet and gets stronger and stronger.

In the following chapters you will learn how to fill crystals with specific magickal intention. When you need a bit of luck or are nervous about a presentation or exam, for example, hold your lucky crystal or wear it as jewelry and say in your mind the magick words you filled it with. The luck and confidence will pulse through you like an electric charge. And, of course, you can fill your crystal charm with protection too.

> ✳ **Tip:** Pointed crystals will scratch other crystals if they are kept in a bag, so be sure to keep these separated from your rounded crystals.

CHAPTER 2
THE BASICS

There are fifteen basic polished stones that you can use for almost everything. Over time you can add other inexpensive but beautiful crystals to your collection, as each one has its own magickal meaning and use.

If you can't afford or are having difficulty finding all fifteen at first, start with the ones marked with a star, or choose a crystal of the same color.

You can keep these basic crystals in a glass bowl on your crystal altar or put them in a drawstring bag when you want to pick one or more out to answer your questions. Sometimes you'll want to choose a single one to tell you about the day ahead.

CHOOSING YOUR SET OF CRYSTALS

Visit a crystal shop, new age, or gift store and pass your writing hand a few inches over a tray of crystals of one kind. You will *know* which one is for you. You can also buy crystals online and make them yours.

Take advantage of field trips or summer camp visits. Museums often sell local tumblestone crystals as well as unpolished gems in rocks that are fabulous for extra power. But keep your eyes open on wilderness, ocean, or forest trips for the glint of crystal in an ordinary rock. You can discover fossils on the shore too.

1. Clear Quartz*

A clear quartz is perfect for just about everything whenever you want some extra oomph, to be noticed in a good way, or to be thought of as a leader or go-getter.

In fortune-telling clear quartz means, *definitely yes, or, go for it now. Aim high; think big; wishes do come true if you want them enough and are ready to go all out.*

Choose a pointed clear quartz to use as an instant magick wand as well as a round or oval one for fortune-telling.

2. Moonstone

Good for calling love with someone special and to stop nightmares. It helps young women get in tune with moods and their menstrual cycle and helps men to explore their gentler magickal side. Use also for safe travel, especially overseas. Moonstone is a powerful anti-spook crystal, good for all moon magick, and good protection against people who try to con you. You can also place it under your pillow to encourage restful sleep.

In fortune-telling, moonstone says, *trust yourself and watch out for dishonest people. Avoid being tempted to take the easy way out or being influenced into doing what you know will bring trouble.*

Some people believe moonstones will get brighter through the month until the moon is full.

3. Red Jasper*

Good for strength, stamina, and physical fitness. It acts as a charm for competing in sports or trying exciting physical activities. Use it for making changes, such as no longer hanging around with people who don't make you happy. It also gives courage to stand up to bullies and sends negativity back to the sender. This is also a great stone to use in healing.

In fortune-telling, red jasper says, *be brave, stand up to anyone who tries to scare you on- or offline; speak out calmly but firmly against anyone who tries to bully you or shout you down.*

4. Carnelian

For independence, whether you are leaving home, or asking for more freedom to stay out late or to go away with friends for the weekend. It stops you feeling guilted by warring parents who are asking you to choose. Carnelian brings confidence to perform publicly, to speak out in class or debates, and to make new friends. It also guides you to the right vacation job, work experience, or internship.

In fortune-telling, carnelian says, *it is all about you. You don't need the approval of friends, teachers, or parents if you have decided what you want to do and be; don't let anyone put you down. You shouldn't feel you have to see people when it suits them or hang around the in-crowd waiting to be included. Live your own way.*

5. Citrine*

Citrine makes you feel happy and loved. It is also good for studying and getting money in a hurry (ask for an increase in allowance in return for extra chores, for this is the bargaining crystal). Yellow citrine brings happy days out with your friends, meeting a smart but fun new boy/girlfriend if you want one, and protection against bullies on- and offline.

In fortune-telling, citrine says, *use your head not your heart; think before taking a risk in life or in love. Try new activities, visit new places, and make friends with new people. Be prepared to move fast once you have decided what to do because opportunities won't wait forever.*

6. Aventurine

The good luck crystal (especially when three are carried in a little bag), it protects against accidents of all kinds. Green aventurine is another crystal for finding love. It inspires brilliant ideas and so is a crystal to carry at school. It brings out your natural charisma and radiance when you go out.

In fortune-telling, aventurine says, *this will be a lucky day when everything will turn out well, and even difficult people will be especially helpful; smile, speak out, and whomever you talk to, you will get a very good response. Enter a competition or audition for a TV show.*

7. Turquoise

If you are stuck on an art or creative writing project, turquoise breaks through the blocks. When attached to a collar, bridle, or cage, turquoise prevents pets from straying or being stolen. It also stops horses from stumbling or getting out of control. Carry turquoise when you have to talk to authority, whether the principal, the law, or when making a bid for leadership. Take turquoise on a driving test so the instructor knows you know what you are doing. It protects against jealousy and what used to be called the "evil eye of envy": folks who hate you just because you do well.

In fortune-telling, turquoise says, *you are a leader, not a follower; you can make a good impression today if you make sure those in authority are listening; don't let jealousy shake you. Stand tall and proud and show you are a force to be reckoned with and your opinion should be taken seriously.*

8. Lapis Lazuli*

This stone is good for not accepting the blame for something that is not your fault. It protects you against brothers or sisters who are always getting you into trouble and stepparents who favor their own children over you. At school lapis lazuli guards against those who steal your ideas and accuse you of copying and against teachers who constantly pick on you. Lapis lazuli helps you to express yourself clearly and calmly, especially if others tease you. Carry one when auditioning for starring roles in any performances or auditions.

In fortune-telling, lapis lazuli says, *time to have a heart-to-heart with a friend, family member, boy/girlfriend, or your guidance counselor if things are not going well; insist on your right to be noticed as a rising star, especially if you feel different or excluded; aim high and show your special, unique talents.*

9. Sodalite

Sodalite is a feel-good crystal that promises slow but sure steps to reach your dreams. Listen to the older folk in the family because they really have done it all before and can help you avoid making big mistakes; hold sodalite on takeoff and landing if you are scared of flying.

In fortune-telling, sodalite says, *stick with old friends or a boy/girlfriend you can trust, rather than dumping them for someone new but unreliable. Put in the hard work now, and you will get your reward before too long.*

10. Amethyst*

A purple amethyst is good for fear and stress. Carry for keeping a low profile. Amethyst guards against spooks and bullies; prevents nightmares; stops cravings for too much junk food; and is excellent for developing your psychic powers and fortune-telling gifts.

In fortune-telling, amethyst says, *wait before jumping in with both feet. Step back from other people's quarrels because if you try to help, you'll only end up getting blamed by all sides.*

11. Tiger's-eye*

Good for success in every way. It encourages saving and getting money through unexpected opportunities. Tiger's-eye sends back all bad-wishing and nastiness coming your way from "friends" who are gossiping behind your back; protects against nasty spirits; and overcomes rivals. Use it to overcome fear of failure.

In fortune-telling, golden brown tiger's-eye says, *look out for any chances today to shine; do not listen to rumors or gossip or those who try to turn you against other people; watch out for those who sabotage your efforts to shine.*

12. Rose Quartz*

This is the good fairy crystal, attracting and keeping love

you can trust, bringing good friends and family happiness, and healing broken hearts. It is the best crystal for mending quarrels between those you care for and also for bringing peace between warring family members; like amethyst, it brings peaceful sleep and beautiful dreams; it's good for making you feel beautiful.

In fortune-telling, rose quartz says, *you may need to keep the peace, either within your family or among friends; time to make up after a stupid quarrel; smile because you are looking good, whatever you've been told by your so-called friends.*

13. Smoky Quartz*

Put smoky quartz in a bag with your smartphone, your tablet, or anything precious, as it keeps away thieves and hackers. It also prevents accidents and protects you day and night against danger and from spirits sent to scare you; good for amazing dreams where you can go anywhere in your sleep. It helps you overcome unhappiness or depression if you hold it up to light. Have one in the car for safety while driving. Smoky quartz reverses bad luck or obstacles if you point it down to the earth outdoors and let anything bad drain through.

In fortune-telling, smoky quartz promises, *today will be better than yesterday, and tomorrow even better; hang in there if you feel the whole world is against you; indulge yourself, it's time for candy and cake.*

14. Hematite

Good for protection against friends and family who drain you with their guilt trips. Hematite brings the truth to light if you have been unfairly accused. Hematite is called the lawyer's stone. This is helpful if your divorcing folks are battling it out in court, so you get your say as to where you live. Hematite is the stone of bringing out hidden talents and of standing up for causes that mean a lot to you. A natural magnet, hematite draws love, success, or whatever you most wish for.

In fortune-telling, hematite says, *don't be modest about your abilities and achievements. Go for recognition and deserved praise; apply for vacation jobs or to join a team as your profile is high. Wear hematite jewelry set in copper (the metal of Venus) for beautiful romance.*

15. Black Onyx*

Good for quitting bad habits and overcoming phobias; for letting people go who are making you unhappy. Onyx gives focus for dealing with chaos and unfinished projects. It is a crystal associated with wizards, witches, and protection against bad magick and people who wish you harm. It is also a powerful wish crystal if you breathe on it three times and fill it with your wishes; it protects you against undesirables on the internet.

In fortune-telling, onyx says, *don't give in to temptation or follow friends you know will get you into trouble; watch out for new friends on social media who may not be who they say.*

GETTING ANSWERS FAST

Once you have your set of fifteen basic crystals, you can use them to tell you what you need to know about the day ahead or to answer your questions about anything. You just put them all in a bag, shake the bag nine times, and pick a crystal without looking.

Trust the crystals and, in time, you'll get all sorts of ideas, pictures in your mind, and feelings that will show you the best way to go forward.

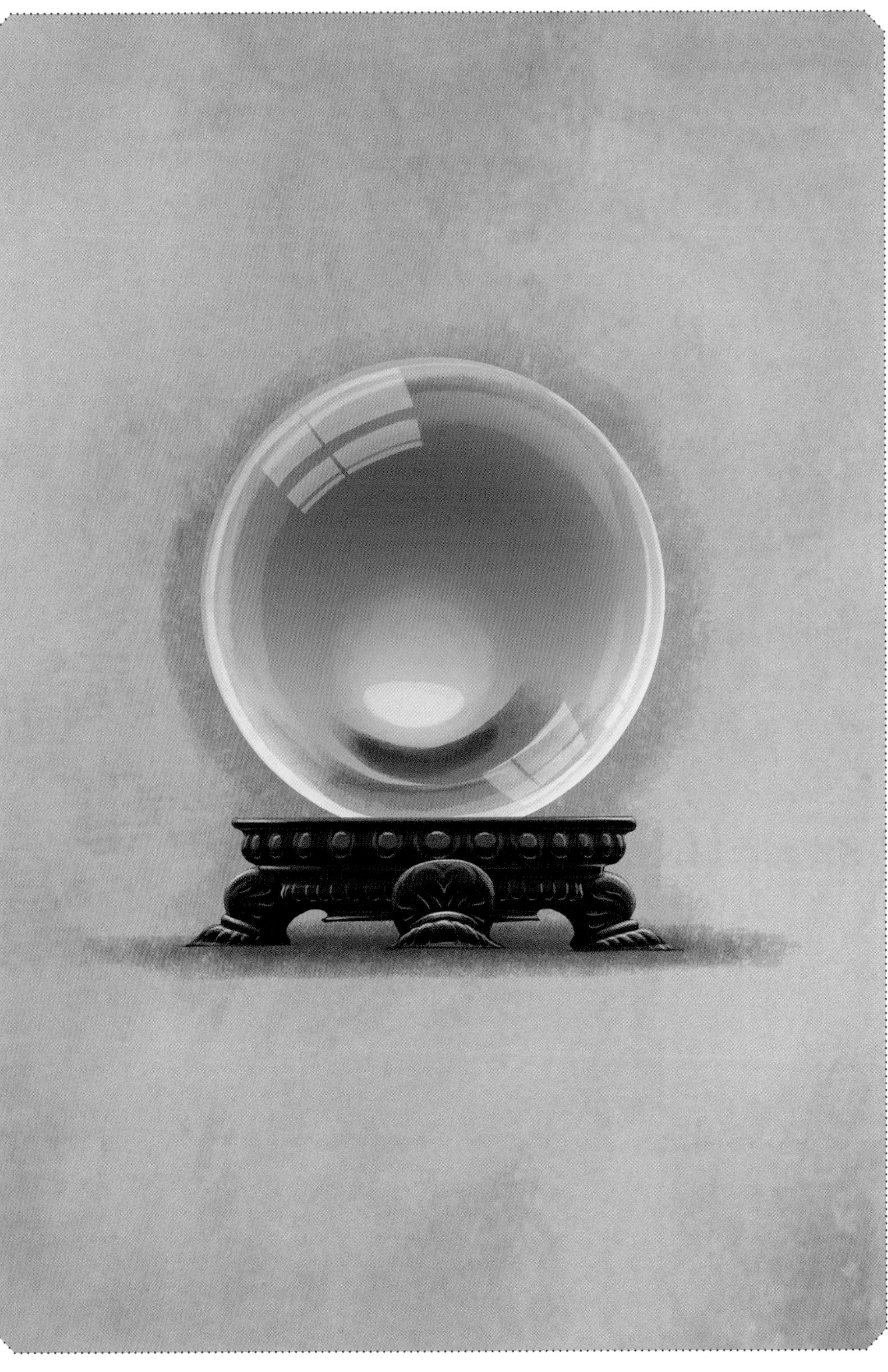

CHAPTER 3

CRYSTAL POWER

Charging crystals is a magickal version of charging your smartphone so it is ready for use. When you buy your crystals, you will want to clear them of the energies of the people who sold them so that they are really tuned in to you. Whenever you want, you can clear a crystal after using it (especially if you choose a different crystal to take with you each day).

These are some of the best ways of clearing your crystals:

USING LIGHT

Place your crystals in a circle around a white or gold candle. Let the candle burn away, and your crystals will be filled with light. You can leave a single crystal in candlelight the same way.

USING WATER

Wash each crystal under a running tap. Do not wash any crystals that are delicate, like selenite or turquoise, or metallic stones, like hematite or lapis lazuli. Leave crystals to dry naturally.

USING MOTHER EARTH

Rest your crystal/s on a small plate on the earth or in a large plant pot for twenty-four hours.

USING FRAGRANCE

Circle a lemongrass, pine, juniper, frankincense, lavender, or rose incense stick nine times counterclockwise in spirals around your crystals. Leave the incense near the crystals to burn through.

USING SALT

Though often a popular method of clearing them, burying your crystals in salt can scratch them. Instead, rest them on a plate on top of a bowl of salt for twenty-four hours.

USING A CRYSTAL PENDULUM

Pass a clear quartz pendulum over crystals in slow counter-clockwise circles nine times and then nine times the other way to give them power. You can use a crystal pendant on a chain if you don't yet have a pendulum.

YOUR CRYSTAL WAND

To fill your crystals with power, you will need a clear quartz crystal magick wand. You can use your pointed quartz if it is long enough to use for circling and pointing. Sometimes new age stores will try to sell you really expensive crystal wands, claiming they have all kinds of amazing powers, but the real power comes from working with your crystals, regardless of price.

You can also make your own wand with a smooth and varnished stick. Make it the length of your forearm, wrist to elbow, with a quartz point attached to one end (cut a groove and glue it in).

CHARGING YOUR CRYSTAL WAND

1. Pick up the wand in your non-writing hand and hold it upright, point at the top. With the index figure of the other hand, press gently on the top of the crystal wand until you feel a gentle throbbing or warmth in your finger.
2. Say, *"I ask that this crystal wand will become magickally mine, used always for the greatest good and in love and healing."*
3. Now breathe softly three times down the length of the wand, and it is charged.

RECHARGING WITH YOUR WAND

1. Put the crystals you are recharging in a circle with your pointed clear quartz wand in the center for a few minutes.
2. Then, going clockwise around the circle with your wand held in your writing hand, touch each crystal with the pointed end of your wand.
3. If you are charging a single crystal, place the wand in front of it, point facing it, for a few more minutes.
4. Afterward, holding your wand so the point is upright, say, *"I fill my crystals with power, I fill you with healing, I fill you with the protection of the spirits to tell me true and guide me with your wisdom."* When you have finished, pass the wand three times clockwise outside the crystals.
5. Your crystals are now ready.

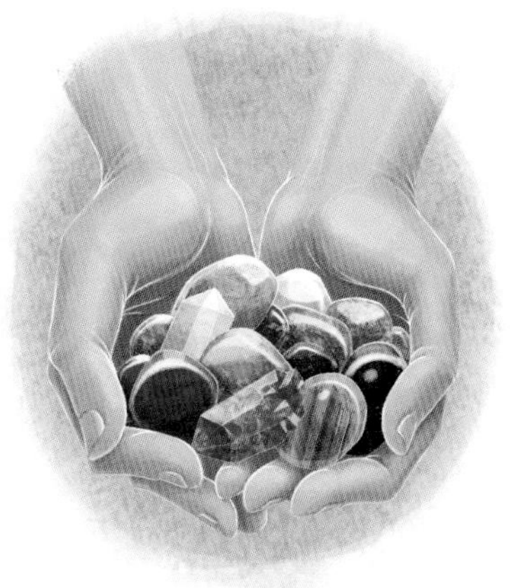

CHAPTER 4

THE CRYSTAL RAINBOW

Each crystal color has a special meaning and power. In addition, a bright, sparkling, or vibrant shade of crystal fills you with *go for it* energies as you hold it, where a softer, gentler shade, even of the same color, calms you.

Some colors, such as red, orange, and yellow, are naturally hot and dynamic, where greens, blues, and purples are softer and calmer. To test this, hold a gleaming red stone in either hand and a soft green stone in the other. Almost immediately you will feel the dynamic energies of the red and the slow, gentler-flowing power of the green. As you develop this gift of crystal touch over time, you will *feel* the powers contained within different crystals.

As you work with more crystals, you may find the agates always make you feel safe and jaspers are strong while the quartzes, even the gentler ones like rose quartz, have a buzz like a very mild electric charge.

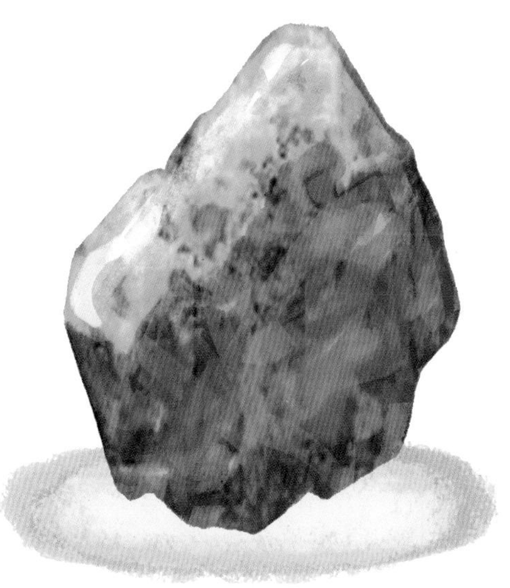

COLOR YOUR LIFE

Now we are going to add to your crystal collection. Two crystals for each color have been suggested so that you can choose one you like and build up your crystal rainbow in your own time. You don't have to buy them all at once, just choose one in your favorite color. You'll already have quite a lot of colors to choose from in your first fifteen.

When you buy a new crystal, write its meaning in your journal. Take a picture of it and place it in your journal, noting what you feel as you use it.

Keep your new rainbow crystals in a second bowl on your crystal altar. When you are fortune-telling, choose from your fifteen crystals first. Then close your eyes and mix the new rainbow crystals still in their bowl. Let your hand pick one; it will add an extra message to your crystal readings. You will always choose the one you need from this second bowl, no matter how many or few you are using.

RED

• action • strength and stamina in physical activities • standing up calmly but firmly against bullies • tackling fears head-on • taking the direct route • speaking openly rather than bottling up your feelings • love • following a passionate interest or talent • success in competitions • standing up against unfairness •

Red Tiger's-eye

Banded gleaming reds.

• to get yourself and others moving • getting past obstacles • determination • stopping bullies • getting yourself noticed and your efforts rewarded • for sending spite right back •

In fortune-telling, red tiger's-eye says, *stand firm and respond coolly but don't back down from any prejudice or unfairness that stops you from being and doing what you want.*

Garnet

Deep or lighter shades of red, in rough cut as well as gem.

• protection against people who take advantage of you • stops anxiety especially if you are away from home or with people you don't know • helps if you are being pressured to achieve or meet deadlines • turning anger into making a positive change • protects against people making you feel guilty or like a failure •

In fortune-telling, red garnet says, *ask for loyalty from your friends or boy/girlfriend, and don't accept second-best treatment. Say what you feel is unfair before it spirals out of control.*

ORANGE

• liking who you really are and not always trying to please others • not doing what others want in order to be popular • letting your creative and artistic side out to play •

Amber

Fossilized tree resin, usually about 30–50 million years old, which has a rich vibrant color and may contain a fossilized leaf or insect.

• to soften people who are stubborn, overcompetitive, or unfriendly • increases your natural beauty and charisma • helps if you are naturally shy • brings memories of past lives if you hold it up to soft sunlight and find the doorway inside it • attracts love and money •

In fortune-telling, amber says, *know you are beautiful/attractive as you are; don't let anyone make you feel you don't belong; take up an activity you enjoy, even if other people don't get it.*

Orange Calcite

Different shades of orange, dark to light, either smooth or glassy, like ice.

• trying again if you have been rejected or things didn't work out • soothes if your hormones are going crazy • healing if you have been abused by anyone, physically or emotionally • creating a relaxed, fun atmosphere when you invite people over • getting people off their smartphones to talk • to relax nervous pets or to settle rescue animals •

In fortune-telling, orange calcite says, *believe in yourself and don't waste time with people who make fun of you; don't be shy in talking to someone you would like as a friend or more, as they may be shy too.*

YELLOW

• for bringing sunshine and happiness into your life • for swiftness and intelligence • for cutting through lies, flattery, and flirtation • protects against human snakes • makes study and memorizing easier • technological wizardry • for using your head rather than your heart • opportunities for moneymaking •

Mustard or Sandy Yellow Jasper

• eases worries about what other people say and think about you • overcomes embarrassment about performing in front of a crowd • for safety on vacation • stops former friends from spreading lies • protects against an online smear campaign by a jealous rival • helps in creating your own space if you share a bedroom, apartment, or dorm •

In fortune-telling, yellow jasper says, *finish any assignments that you have been putting off, and spring clean your room and life; get rid of activities and people you no longer want to be with; time to shine in performances or auditions.*

Lemon Chrysoprase

Lemon yellow to yellow-green, can be slightly sparkly.

• for keeping away spite, gossip, lies, and pettiness • protects against rivals • keeps you safe if you are always getting in trouble with authority figures • stops you from being influenced by peer pressure • put under a pet bed to stop existing pets from being jealous of a new arrival • helps you think fast and argue eloquently under pressure • see through deception in others •

In fortune-telling, lemon chrysoprase says, *do not be tempted to cut corners, whether in homework or chores; don't do harmful things, even if friends are trying to persuade you; beware of a false friend; double-check what you have been told about someone you know.*

GREEN

• trusting your heart and not your head • good luck • improving in something without major stress if you are patient •

Malachite

Emerald to grass green with black or pale green stripes, bands, or swirls.

• resisting people who make you feel responsible for their happiness • protecting you from online trolls • stopping nasty texts and calls to your smartphone • put next to your bedroom computer if you just can't switch it off at night • good luck •

In fortune-telling, malachite says, *follow your heart; don't let anyone influence you because you feel sorry for them; if you feel sad or worried, do something to make yourself happy; stay away from those whose moans and complaints bring you down.*

Jade

There are two different kinds, nephrite and jadeite, but they are similar with colors ranging from deep green to bright green to very pale green.

• protects you from violence in your neighborhood, school, or home • for new romance, faithful and lasting love, and finding a soul mate when the time is right • keeps you safe when casting magick spells • drives away deceitful spirits • called the "gardener's crystal," as it makes everything grow in your life: friendship, popularity, love • protects anyone in the hospital • guards you if you are accident-prone • soothes old or sick pets •

In fortune-telling, jade says, *don't give up just because results are slow in coming; work on an existing friendship or love that has lost its sparkle; trust your instincts as to whether someone new on- or offline is trustworthy.*

BLUE

• for training and long-term learning • helps you handle difficult or boring study • following necessary rules and going through official channels when things seem unfair • passing examinations •

Blue Lace Agate

Pale blue, sometimes brighter blue with white or brown threads of color.

• calming stress • speaking clearly if you stumble over words • gives you patience if you help care for an elderly, sick, or disabled relative • for good relationships with your grandma and mom • connects you with your spirit guides • peace and quiet • for world peace, put blue lace agate on pictures of war-torn places and of any military personnel you know in order to keep them safe •

In fortune-telling, blue lace agate says, *beware of backstabbers and those who spread rumors about others (you could be next); don't be tempted to act as peacemaker in friends' rivalries, as they may blame you for their problems; speak the truth always but with kindness.*

PURPLE

• peaceful sleep, beautiful dreams • magick and good witchcraft • for quiet activities with a few good friends • to step back if the world is whizzing by too fast • reconnecting with friends and family members • protection physically, mentally, emotionally, and psychically from harm •

Purple Fluorite

Choose a different shade of purple than your amethyst. Purple fluorite, which looks like glass, comes in all shades, from pale lavender to violet.

• overcoming panic • protection from ghosts • for making assignments, exams, and interviews much easier • for problems with hyperactivity or ADHD • attach to a pet collar when training a young dog or horse • a reality check for anyone who is happier daydreaming than facing the everyday world • shields you from feeling nervous during medical tests •

Sugilite

Lilac to violet with black markings; it can be quite expensive but is well worth asking for as a gift.

• protects against jealousy • stops you from feeling nervous when meeting new people or going to new places • prevents teasing by others • comforting if your parents are divorced or separated and you are feeling lost or torn in two directions • for meditation •

In fortune-telling, sugilite says, *It's not what you have or can afford that matters but who you are and your kindness to others; you may come across an environmental cause or a situation where you can make a positive difference to others.*

WHITE

Contains all the other rainbow colors

• brings success in any way you want • grants wishes • offers health, happiness, and the *get up and go* vibe • helps to bring fun, adventure, and excitement every day •

Howlite

Bright white with gray or white veins in a weblike pattern.

• physical health and fitness: offers stamina and determination if you've hit your limit physically or emotionally • helps you stick to studying when there are distractions • for completing homework where detail is necessary • defuses stress • on an animal collar or beneath the pet bed encourages wandering animals, especially cats, not to stray • brings success in art or music • under your pillow reduces fears of the dark •

In fortune-telling, howlite says, *you may need to touch home base for a while; spend time in familiar places with friendly faces if you are feeling jittery or have had a tough time; don't skimp on details, as everything may take twice as long as it should.*

Selenite or Satin Spar

White with pearl-like sheen, very similar to its sister, satin spar, which has a shimmering stripe around it.

• for wishes when held under the full moon • brings good luck • helps concentration if you are smart but just can't focus • relaxes and calms you • protects the home and family • takes away fear of the dark, especially if you are away from home • for moon spells and love and romance magick •

In fortune-telling, selenite says, *make up following a quarrel with someone who has behaved stupidly, but you may have to make the first move; try to organize some family time and outings even if everyone is busy.*

CHAPTER 5

THE REST OF THE RAINBOW

Now you are working with the seven-color crystal rainbow. But there are other colors that are full of really useful powers! You can add one or more of these to your bowl of rainbow crystals. Don't feel like you need to buy them all at once. Just add crystals to your rainbow crystal bowl as you get them. Shop around if you can. Often a crystal stall in a market or fair will have really beautiful crystals at a fraction of the price you'll pay in a new age store. They don't need to be gem quality. A rough-cut garnet is just as powerful as a gem garnet. If you have birthstone jewelry, you can make it into a personal traveling powerhouse.

PINK

Pink is linked magickally with green and deals with matters of the heart.

• quiet sleep and peaceful dreams • for overcoming issues around food • forgiving someone who has wronged you • taking care of anyone younger, sick, or afraid • first love and gentle romance • happiness with family and friends • making your room special, even if you share it • overcoming hormonal swings • caring for pregnant animals, small creatures, and young pets •

Mangano or Pink Calcite

Very pale pink with white bands or spots.

• sending love to a sick relative or pet, or a place in need • overcoming shyness • protects against bad ghosts • links you with your guardian angels, fairies, and nature spirits • helpful if you are in foster care, or are adopted and are having problems finding your birth mother • comforting if you are feeling homesick or there are changes in your home life •

In fortune-telling, mangano calcite says, *talk over any worries with family or friends; if they can't help, find a sympathetic counselor. If your life is good someone close will need you to listen to their problems but may not like to ask.*

Rhodonite

Reddish to salmon or rose pink with black patches and veins.

• to get over love that is not returned • helps to control your temper • protects against online fraud • to improve things if you or someone else is disabled or ill and not getting help that is needed • to learn to love yourself and value your own company rather than dashing into the wrong friendships or love relationships • to get your talent recognized • keep under your pillow to avoid psychic attacks and to get you up on time •

In fortune-telling, rhodonite says, *don't make the same mistakes again; avoid people who bring out the worst in you or get you into trouble; take time for yourself, as you may be giving too much time to others.*

BROWN

• for getting to work and not dreaming your life away • resisting a quick fix or taking shortcuts that carry risks • patience if you're not getting the recognition you'd like • saving and not spending • spending time with older family members • taking care of old pets • succeeding through hard work •

You already have gleaming golden-brown tiger's-eye in your set of fifteen, but most brown crystals are more matte in color, so they release their energies more gradually.

Banded Agate

Bands of different browns and fawns, sometimes with an eye shape in the center.

• overcoming fixation on an unrealistic love • being sensible with money • living harmoniously with many family members • handling part-time/temporary job as well as school work • memorizing boring but necessary facts • soothing old or very sick pets • protecting you from any attack, earthly or paranormal •

In fortune-telling, brown banded agate says, *remember Rome wasn't built in a day, so don't give up if getting where you want is taking forever: choose the safe route to success and happiness even if it takes longer.*

Rutilated Quartz

Clear quartz packed with brownish gold needles. This stone is also found with gold- and copper-colored needles. The more golden your rutiles, the more dynamic the crystal. Every rutilated quartz is believed to contain a guardian spirit who will always keep you safe.

• for bringing out talents, especially if you fear you have fallen behind classmates • protection against black magic and dark spirits • helps you gain a place in the right educational or career path • to ignore a spiteful person •

In fortune-telling, rutilated quartz says, *start a new activity or join that group, club, or team you thought you weren't smart or popular enough to try; revive a talent or two from your childhood.*

GRAY

• avoiding entering arguments you can't win • keeping a low profile and don't get caught up in trouble • protecting you against psychic attack • keeping secrets •

You should definitely consider getting a second hematite for your rainbow bowl as this is a powerful protective crystal and good for getting what you want.

Labradorite

Gray crystal with iridescent flashes or patches of red, blue, green, gold, and silver.

• brings out your hidden gifts • offers time out from the noise of others • protective for night driving • helps you to break bad habits and get away from bad influences • takes away fears and anxiety • good for clairvoyance and developing psychic powers • protects computer files, especially those stored online • prevents mistakes when working online • helps with healing •

In fortune-telling, labradorite says, *avoid being the referee in other people's arguments; you may have to temporarily make the best of a less than ideal situation, but soon you will be able to do things your way. You will feel your spirit guardians guiding and protecting you.*

BLACK

• absorbing all sorrow, nastiness, and fears • letting go of a friendship or relationship that isn't working • for moving on to a new location or career/study option • energy to continue trying if you keep hitting a brick wall • protection against internet frauds and predators • quitting bad habits and people who lead you astray •

Obsidian

Dark, usually black volcanic glass through which you can see the light; the more transparent form is called Apache Tears.

• good times coming after bad • helps relieve depression and phobias • dealing with grief after a death or separation in your life • protection against people who are constantly demanding your time and attention • a small obsidian arrow in your workspace facing inward protects you from gossip or spite, while pointing outward calls in new chances after a big setback • placed beneath a pet bed, obsidian relaxes a nervous, highly strung pet •

In fortune-telling, obsidian says, *avoid emotional vampires and over-possessive people who try to run your life; don't be afraid to change the rules in love or friendship if you do all the giving.*

Schorl or Black Tourmaline

Black and shiny, sometimes with lines down it.

• for overcoming anxiety, self-harming, and panic attacks • protects against cyberattacks of all kinds and viciousness on social media • assists concentration • wakes up a sleepy mind • guards against nasty neighbors • stops you from feeling spooked in dark or scary places •

For fortune-telling, black tourmaline says, *you should stop worrying as everything will turn out right; clear hangers-on from your life who keep you away from your real friends.*

CHAPTER 6
CRYSTAL READINGS

CHOOSING THE RIGHT CRYSTAL EVERY DAY

For fortune-telling you can put all your crystals, or as many as you like, in a purse or drawstring bag so you can select the right one/s by touch. You can also pick a single crystal from your bag of crystals each day (without looking). It will not only tell you what you need to know for the day ahead, it will also act as a protector and good-luck charm. Take it with you in a little bag or purse. Touch it inside the tiny bag during the day when you need some confidence or protection. Your angels will guide you to pick the right crystal. You can also sleep with the chosen crystal under your pillow to bring answers in your dreams or to keep you safe.

Ask as you pick, morning or evening, that you will choose the crystal for what you most want or need. You may find that you pick the same crystal day after day. The universe is saying, *"Hey, pay attention, this is a message you need to hear loud and clear."*

As well as the fortune-telling messages listed previously, you can hold your crystal and let your wise angels show you pictures in your mind, and maybe words too.

You have already created your crystal altar and started picking both a crystal every day and two or three to answer your questions from your bag of fifteen crystals. Below you will find a method to help you answer questions for yourself and others by choosing up to six crystals from your bag of fifteen.

If you are unsure of the meanings, make a list of the fifteen crystals and just one line about them each to refer to until you feel sure of the meanings.

Ask the blessings of the angels or your special guardians before the reading begins.

How to Read Crystals

1. Put your fifteen crystals in a bag and, holding the bag, ask your question or that of the person you are reading for aloud.
2. If reading for another person, ask them to feel inside the bag and pick three crystals, one after the other. Use six crystals if the question is complicated.
3. Now ask the person to gently throw the crystals from their cupped hands onto a small table you set up prior to the reading, covered with a scarf or cloth of your choice.
4. If any crystals fall on the floor, put them back in the bag and ask the questioner to choose crystals again to make three in total on the table. If necessary, continue putting floor crystals back in the bag till three or six are on the cloth. If reading for yourself, you would, of course, choose and cast the crystals onto the table.
5. Now pick up and hold each crystal in turn, starting with the one closest to the center of the table. With your eyes closed allow your fingertips to absorb feelings and ideas from each

stone. This might appear as pictures in your mind, words, or just feelings. Then use the meaning of the color and kind of crystal for guidance.

6. Explain the meanings if you are reading for someone else and add what you saw, heard, and felt when you held each crystal.
7. Afterward, ask the person to hold the crystals in open-cupped hands and see if anything new is coming through to explain things that weren't clear. You can also talk together about what the crystals are saying so the answer becomes clear.
8. If you also have a bowl of rainbow crystals you have collected, ask the person you are reading for to close their eyes and pick one or two. Add their meanings to the reading as you hold them. Do this yourself for your own readings.
9. At the end of the reading thank your angels or guardians. Don't forget to cleanse your crystals afterward.

Note: If two or more crystals are clustered together, this indicates the meanings will be connected, especially when you are using six crystals in the cast. If one crystal is on its own, ask the questioner if they feel alone in this matter or if what they want is being opposed.

GINNY'S CRYSTAL READING

Ginny wants to know if she should go on summer vacation with her family to their beach house by the ocean. She has been going since she was small, but now Ginny is sixteen and has been asked to help on an inner-city summer sports project by her best friend, Becky.

Ginny picks a carnelian, a rose quartz, and a red jasper.

Carnelian is the stone of independence and not being pressured into doing what you don't want to do. Ginny loves her family dearly but says that sometimes they treat her as if she is five. They worry when she wants to go away without them, and she has turned down other trips.

The *red jasper* right next to it in the center of the table is for action, courage, and sporting activities. Ginny says when she holds the red jasper, she is reminded she always wanted to be a sports coach. Ginny wants to work with under priviledged children after she graduates in the future. The summer sports project is a chance to see if she enjoys this kind of work.

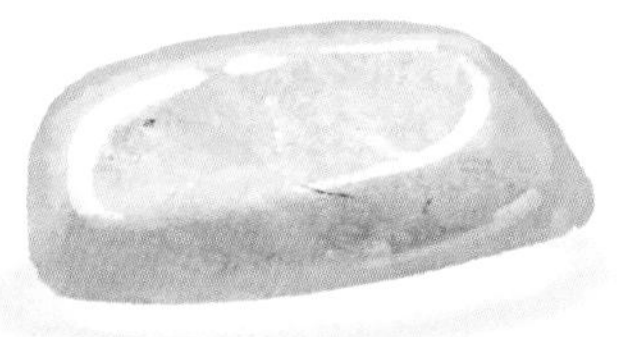

Rose quartz, by itself at the edge of the table, shows the dilemma. Ginny loves going to the ocean with all her cousins and knows how disappointed her mother will be. But this is such a good opportunity, and Ginny can reassure her mom she will be well cared for by Becky's family.

Ginny decides she can't turn down the summer project and that she will ask Becky's mother to talk to her mother.

The Result

Ginny had a brilliant summer on the project. Yes, she missed the ocean vacation like crazy. But she now knows in which direction her future will go, and Ginny's family is very proud of her.

USING YOUR CRYSTALS FOR SPECIAL WISHES

If you have an urgent wish or need, you can use your crystal altar to create the necessary powers.

Whatever your need, you can charge your crystal altar for up to a week before the big event using any of your crystals to build up the luck, love, or success needed. You can use different crystals for different parts of the need.

- Check the color meanings in the previous chapters.
- You might choose a blue crystal for examination success, and yellow for study and remembering the facts or steps in an exam.
- For a college acceptance you would use blue for long-term training and maybe green for good luck.
- Change the candle in the center for one that's the same color as the crystal, or use two candles if you decide to use two different crystals.
- Use an incense stick in frankincense for success; rose for love, friendship, family, and popularity; lavender for travel or study; and sandalwood for money and career.

The Ritual

1. Put the incense in a holder to the right of the candle. Set a bowl of water to the left of the candle. Put your one or two crystals in the center. Leave your crystal wand in your crystal place in front of the crystals, pointed end facing them to draw in power.
2. Light your candles left to right and your incense stick from each candle in turn.

3. Touch each crystal in turn (if you are using more than one) with the pointed end of your wand saying, *"I fill you with power for (name, purpose, and the date you need the help)."*
4. When you have finished, pass the wand three times around the outside of the crystal/s in a clockwise circle, saying the same words three times.
5. Holding the incense stick like a pen, spiral the smoke in the air around the outside of the crystals three times, saying the words again three times.
6. Sprinkle drops of water from your water bowl three times in a circle clockwise around the crystals, saying the same words three times more.
7. Blow out the candle/s and leave the incense to burn.
8. Leave the crystals and wand in place. Each day touch each crystal with the pointed end of the wand and repeat the words three times.
9. On the morning of the event put the crystal/s in a small bag or purse and take it with you.

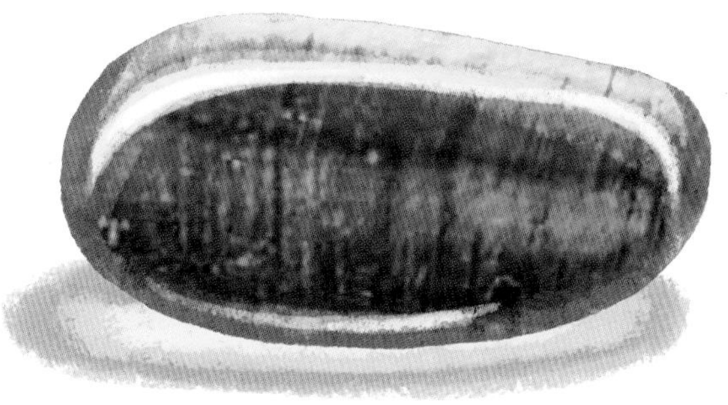

CHAPTER 7

BIRTH MONTH AND ZODIAC CRYSTALS AND GEMS

You may already have found your favorite crystal and are using your basic fifteen crystals regularly, along with your rainbow crystals, for fortune-telling, but there are even more personal crystals you can discover.

Your zodiac stones and birthstones are especially lucky for you whenever you need an extra rush of power or success. They also radiate to show the world that you like yourself for who you are as you are. The power of zodiac stones and gems keeps growing the more you wear or carry them.

ZODIAC CRYSTALS IN ACTION

Each zodiac sign has its own crystals and gems. If you are given a jewel for a birthday, holiday, or special event present, they will always call good luck into your life. A tiny precious stone is just as powerful as a large one. You can buy inexpensive rough-cut or tumblestone versions of many precious and semiprecious gems, such as rubies, emeralds, or sapphires, that have the same powers as the cut jewels.

Check out each sign in the list below and on the following pages for magickal properties. If angels aren't for you, picture a guardian in the same colors and with the same zodiac powers.

Write in your crystal journal all the zodiac and birth month crystals, not just your own. Zodiac crystals can be used by anyone, anytime, whenever you need that particular zodiac crystal's power.

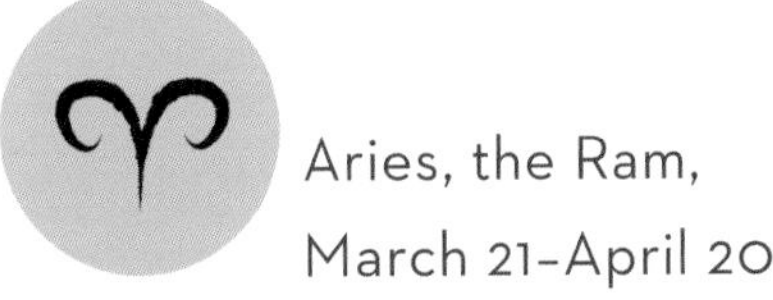

Aries, the Ram, March 21–April 20

Crystals: Blood agate, red carnelian, diamond, red jasper, obsidian (rainbow, silver, or gold sheen), polished silver iron pyrites and polished gold chalcopyrite, rhodonite, red tiger's-eye

Angel: Machidiel, warrior angel

Zodiac strengths: Self-confidence, strong sense of who you are, originality, assertiveness, action, courage, competitiveness, determination

Zodiac weaknesses: Anger over small things, bossiness, selfishness

Color: Red

Taurus, the Bull, April 21–May 21

Crystals: Pink/mango calcite, green chrysoprase, emerald, jade, rainbow moonstone, pink Andean opal, rhodochrosite, rose quartz, pink tourmaline

Angel: Asmodel, angel of beauty

Zodiac strengths: Persistence, patience, loyalty, ability to get things done, loving beautiful things, party planning

Zodiac weaknesses: Fear or unwillingness to try new things or meet new people, stubbornness

Color: Pink or pale green

Gemini, the Heavenly Twins,
May 22–June 21

Crystals: Yellow agate, yellow calcite, lemon chrysoprase, citrine, yellow jasper, labradorite, lemon quartz, yellow zircon

Angel: Ambriel the messenger and travel angel

Zodiac strengths: Can talk yourself into or out of anything, fit into any situation or group, scientific/technological know-how, curiosity, intelligence, eager for new experiences, quick to learn when you want to, love of travel and adventure

Zodiac weaknesses: Easily bored or distracted, impatient with people, tendency to exaggerate

Color: Pale yellow/gray

Cancer, the Crab,
June 22–July 22

Crystals: Moonstone, opal, opalite, pearl, cloudy or milky white quartz, satin spar, selenite, clear topaz

Angel: Muriel the silvery and pearl-robed healer angel

Zodiac strengths: Sensitivity, kindness, imagination, love of home and family, ability to keep secrets, quiet sleep

Zodiac weaknesses: Possessiveness, overdependency on home and family, secretiveness

Color: Silver

Leo, the Lion,
July 23–August 23

Crystals: Amber, carnelian, fire opal, fire quartz, rainbow quartz, ruby, white sapphire, sardonyx, red spinel, sunstone

Angel: Verchiel, the golden joy bringer

Zodiac strengths: Power, courage, generosity, leadership, good at public performances

Zodiac weaknesses: Admiting you are wrong, not letting others take the lead

Color: Gold

Virgo, the Maiden, August 24–September 22

Crystals: Moss or tree agate, amazonite, green calcite, white howlite, green garnet, jade, peridot, serpentine, snow quartz

Angel: Hamaliel or Hamaiel, angel of perfection

Zodiac strengths: Wanting to do your best, good at organizing, efficiency, healing powers, ability to carry through a boring but necessary task, reliability

Zodiac weaknesses: Getting upset if you don't always get your way, being stuck in details so you never finish anything, hating other people's noise and mess

Color: Green

Libra, the Scales, September 23–October 23

Crystals: Blue chalcedony, chrysocolla, blue lace agate, lapis lazuli, white or rainbow opal, blue quartz, rubellite/red tourmaline, blue sapphire

Angel: Zuriel, the teacher

Zodiac strengths: Ability to see both sides of an argument, tact, good at making peace, a strong sense of right and wrong, charm

Zodiac weaknesses: Flirting, trying to keep everyone happy

Color: Light blue

Scorpio, the Scorpion, October 24–November 22

Crystals: Hematite, malachite, obsidian, mahogany obsidian, black pearl, titanium aura quartz, red spinel, unakite, red zircon

Angel: Bariel, the angel of small miracles

Zodiac strengths: The ability to

go all out for what you believe in, psychic powers, determination, to start again after a setback

Zodiac weaknesses: Bearing grudges and not letting go of old hurts or love; desire for revenge

Color: Indigo, burgundy red

Sagittarius, The Archer, November 23–December 21

Crystals: Orange aragonite, azurite, chrysocolla, blue goldstone and gold goldstone, blue howlite, aqua aura quartz, clear quartz, golden topaz, turquoise

Angel: Adnachiel or Advachiel, the angel of learning and exploration

Zodiac strengths: Generosity, love of travel and adventure, seeing possibilities in bad situations or people, honesty, lack of prejudice, enthusiasm, creativity, especially in writing

Zodiac weaknesses: Giving up the minute things go wrong or get boring, always wanting new excitement and new people, not finishing anything

Color: Bright yellow

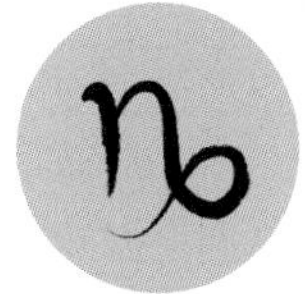

Capricorn, the Goat, December 22–January 20

Crystals: Green aventurine, bronzite, red garnet, onyx, petrified wood, rubellite/red tourmaline, smoky quartz, tiger's-eye, black tourmaline

Angel: Anael or Hanael, the protector and archangel of love and faithfulness

Zodiac strengths: Being careful and sure, persistence regardless of opposition, respect for traditions, ambition, loyalty, good with money, good at resisting pressure

Zodiac weaknesses: Refusal to give up on hopeless situations or people, unable to see anyone else's point of view, unwillingness to have fun, sometimes bad in taking turns to pay

Color: Indigo, Brown

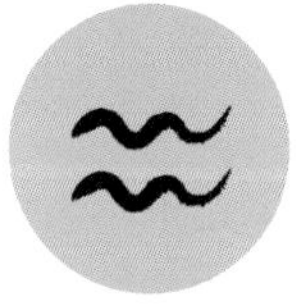

Aquarius, the Water Carrier, January 21–February 18

Crystals: Amethyst, angelite, blue celestite, Andean blue opal, blue quartz, titanium aura quartz, sodalite, blue spinel, sugilite

Angel: Cambiel, who protects you day and night from your own mistakes and all danger

Zodiac strengths: Strong sense of right and wrong, independence, interest in the wider world, wanting to make a difference, inventiveness, not swayed by feelings, lots of interests, totally unique

Zodiac weaknesses: Crankiness if things don't go your way, impatient with sentimental or overemotional people, hating being made to conform

Color: Dark blue, purple

Pisces, the Fish, February 19–March 20

Crystals: Aquamarine, clear aragonite, golden beryl, bloodstone, fluorite, ocean or orbicular jasper, pink and lilac kunzite, mother-of-pearl, watermelon tourmaline

Angel: Barakiel or Barchiel, the archangel of good luck

Zodiac strengths: Very intuitive and psychic, empathy, dreamer and storyteller, an ability to fit in, interest in different kinds of spirituality

Zodiac weaknesses: Getting involved in other people's lives and problems, worrying, expecting too much of people

Color: Soft white, mauve

YOUR BIRTH MONTH CRYSTAL

The magickal powers for each month are especially active if it is your birth month. You can also use a month crystal, even if it is not your birth month crystal, any time during that month if you need its strength or protection.

JANUARY: Red garnet
Qualities: Protection, new beginnings, leaving behind bad habits and fears, mending quarrels

FEBRUARY: Amethyst
Qualities: Balance, new love, increasing good luck, melting coldness, planting the seeds of future success

MARCH: Aquamarine, bloodstone
Qualities: Psychic powers, courage, making the changes you want in your life, action, excelling in new activities

APRIL: Diamond, clear quartz
Qualities: *Go for it* power, believing in yourself, creativity, successful study, making new friends

MAY: Emerald, chrysoprase
Qualities: Love, travel, home and family, giving your room a makeover, getting unexpected help with money

JUNE: Pearl, alexandrite, moonstone
Qualities: Fun, parties and celebrations, doing well at school, or work, joining new clubs

JULY: Ruby, red-brown carnelian
Qualities: Stardom, leadership, success, winning prizes, overcoming shyness

AUGUST: Peridot, sardonyx
Qualities: Persistence, opening doors in your life, reversing bad luck, finding or recovering what is lost

SEPTEMBER: Blue sapphire, lapis lazuli
Qualities: Justice or honesty, success with tests, succeeding in projects and study where learning is hard

OCTOBER: Opal, pink tourmaline
Qualities: Ability to persuade others, success against serious

competition, unexpected invitations, learning new skills and technology

NOVEMBER: Gold topaz, citrine
Qualities: Money, dreams coming true even in small ways, perfecting a skill or talent

DECEMBER: Turquoise, blue or clear topaz, red or blue zircon
Qualities: knowledge and success through learning, completing unfinished ideas and projects

ENCHANTING YOUR ZODIAC AND BIRTHSTONES

Birth month and zodiac stones are very personal to you because they are connected with your date of birth, so this enchantment is a very special way of filling them with power. You have already used your wand to fill crystals with power; this method is very similar, but only uses your hands.

Of course, you can use the enchantment method for absolutely any crystal or group of crystals placed in a circle as well. It is a very gentle method and can be good for fragile crystals such as selenite, any calcite, or fluorite. Gems, crystals, and gem jewelry also tend to be more delicate than solid tumblestones.

Enchantment creates a strong connection between you and your crystal or gem jewelry. It is also very handy if you don't have a candle, incense, or your wand with you. You can do this anywhere if you ever need extra power in your crystal.

1. Set your stones, whether a single crystal, jewelry, or a circle of crystals, flat on any surface.
2. Pass your writing hand clockwise a few inches above the stone/jewelry/circle of crystals nine times.
3. Pass your other hand counterclockwise at the same time in slow circles, palms flat and facing downward and fingers together, nine times.
4. Repeat softly nine times, *"Be for me protection and power, every hour, filled with light, keep me safe by day and night."*

To fill or refill the gem or crystal jewelry with power, breathe in and out gently. Between each breath whisper into the stone how you are seeking its strength or protection.

Each kind of jewelry gives power to a particular part of your body and the magickal energy centers we have within us. You can wear them at different times according to the kind of strength or protection you need. Make a collection of crystal bracelets, earrings, etc.; this need not be expensive. They do not have to be only your own zodiac sign crystals, but any you really like that have meanings that resonate with you.

EARRINGS guard your third, or psychic, eye in the center of your brow. This is where nasty thoughts from others enter and worries keep you awake. In addition, they keep you safe from spooky experiences. They also enhance your psychic abilities, so they are good to wear for crystal readings or for doing magick.

NECKLACES or **PENDANTS** protect your throat energy center from spiteful words and give you the power to say what you want without becoming tongue-tied. They will help you to sound confident and stand out as a natural leader, even if you are quaking in your sneakers.

BRACELETS and **RINGS** shield your sensitive loving heart and also send out *love me, but I'm no pushover* vibes, because your inner wrist pulse points, hands, and fingers are connected to the heart. A necklace or pendant that covers your heart does the same. A friendship or love ring worn on your left ring finger keeps love true; most of all, bracelets and rings help you to love yourself as you are and help you radiate your natural beauty.

A **BELT** with crystals on it or a **CRYSTAL BUCKLE** protects your inner sun center, located at the base and center of your rib cage. It gives you the confidence to make friends with whomever you want; it helps you shine however you choose and also keeps away bullies. A belt also connects with your navel energy place and guards this invisible but important center of fears and feelings; it helps you to ask for what you want from other people and from life.

Because your crystal belt buckle or crystal fastened around your waist is ruled by two psychic centers in your body, it also helps you believe in yourself, whatever anyone says. It reminds you that you can be fit and healthy in the way that is right for you.

ANKLE BRACELETS and **TOE RINGS** offer defense against physical threats or danger, sending out *don't mess with me* vibes. They are also good if you have a tendency to panic, enabling you to walk or run into the world or stand firm and proud, ready for anything.

GIVING YOUR JEWELRY A BIT OF EXTRA OOMPH

Choose which jewelry feels right for different situations. Before putting it on, touch the place you will be wearing it. Then touch each piece of jewelry in turn, asking for whatever you most want from the day/evening ahead. Ask also for any special protection you might need if you know someone spiteful or difficult will be present at the place you are going.

CHAPTER 8

CRYSTAL CHARM BAGS

You may have realized that every time you fill a crystal with power and protection, you are carrying out magick. When you cast a crystal spell to create a magickal crystal charm bag, the power of the whole spell stays in the crystal or bag of crystals afterward. You can also use magick spells to find jewelry with magickal powers. Afterward, just by touching the bag or wearing the jewelry, you are triggering the spell, which is like casting it again. This offers a boost of a power or protection.

If you don't feel spells are for you, you don't have to do them; you can stick to enchantment. But try a spell, and you'll find you are quickly hooked.

MAKING CRYSTAL CHARM BAGS

You can use three, five, seven, nine, or thirteen crystals. These are traditional numbers for charm bags, but sometimes, of course, those numbers won't feel right. If that's the case, use the number of crystals that does feel right.

Use a purse of the same color as the wish, or use a gauze or velvet drawstring bag in that color that's big enough to hold your crystals. Refer to PAGES 25–31 for a list of magickal color meanings.

The bags in crystal stores can be a bit pricey. Shop around and check bargain stores that often sell them in packs for wedding or baby shower favors. There is usually a whole rainbow of colors you can stock up on.

CHOOSING THE RIGHT CRYSTALS FOR YOUR CHARM BAGS

You have already learned about a lot of crystals so far in this book, starting with your basic fifteen. It's worth buying extras of these for spell bags. You also have your rainbow crystals as well as your zodiac and birth month crystals to choose from.

There are twelve more crystals you can choose from in this chapter. They are traditionally used in charm bags and magick spells. Most are really useful additions to bags and are quite cheap to buy in the tumblestone variety.

Of course, it will take months, even years, to build up a good collection, but you have several crystals with similar magickal meanings already. If in doubt use one that is the same color as the magickal ones listed below. If not using them in a charm bag, add them to your bowl of rainbow crystals.

Amazonite

Green-blue or turquoise, often with white lines.

• for getting over illness, anxiety, depression, or emotional problems • strength and courage to overcome prejudice, opposition, or unfairness • to be in the right place at the right time for new opportunities and to meet the right person/people •

* Three amazonites in a charm bag bring good fortune for winning competitions and raffles and for any time where a sudden burst of luck is needed.

Ametrine

A mixture of citrine and amethyst in the same stone.

• overcoming bad habits and getting fit and healthy • defeating opposition if your folks have issues with same-sex relationships or gender fluidity •

* Three in a charm bag for times when you need to keep calm but alert, such as everything from exams to making a presentation, competing in sports or talent contests, or standing for leadership
* Use a single amazonite for keeping the peace between family or friends who are always asking you to choose bet ween them.

Angelite

Glacier or lilac blue, sometimes with white veins.

• to fit in socially if you are shy • protective against teasing • if you worry about the way you look or have problems around food or weight issues • to bring out musical gifts •

* Five in a charm bag kept under your pillow at night to take away fear of the dark and keep away unfriendly ghosts.
* Use a single angelite to connect you with your angels and guardians.

Bloodstone

Deep green with red markings.

• lucky for sports matches, physical activities, and all competitions • for winning no matter how hopeless it seems •

- Three in a charm bag to carry with you for courage to stand against bullies.
- Use a single one if teachers or family are pressuring you to work harder and you are doing your best.

Calcite

Pale to mid-green, pale blue or yellow, either smooth or like ice. Calcite comes in many colors, but these are the most useful for magick and easily obtainable.

• attracts money • protects smartphones and tablets from thieves and online trolls • calms nerves • helps to overcome shyness • soothes nervous pets •

- Keep seven small ones in a charm bag tied to a tree in your garden or at the base of a green plant in your room to connect with earth and nature spirits and fairies.
- Use a single one of any color if you are always in a rush or eat too much junk food.

Chrysocolla

Sky blue to blue-green; sometimes blue and green mixed.

• for bringing luck and overcoming nerves at talent shows • dealing with people who throw tantrums and boy/girlfriends who flirt with others • for skill in yoga or Tai Chi • safety while driving •

- Five in a charm bag next to your computer or tablet to protect you from malice via the internet.
- Use a single one to learn new musical instruments, take up singing or drama, and have the confidence to perform in public.
- Bury one near any adjoining fence or boundary if neighbors are always complaining about you.

Chrysoprase

Apple or mint green.

• for successful college or job applications • for all new beginnings • a natural money charm • tunes you in when you are working psychically • helps you to successfully handle food or image issues •

- Five small ones in a charm bag on top of dull projects or piles of unfinished homework or assignments.
- Use a single one to protect against jealous rivals

Dendritic agate

White with feathery green branchlike markings.

• For remembering facts • kept next to your computer, smartphone, or tablet for surfing social media for good friends and people you have lost touch with • for making new friends safely on the internet • protects you when traveling • connects you with your power or spirit animals •

- Three in a charm bag with a photograph of a family member or boy/girlfriend who is overseas or serving with the military and can't get home.

- Use a single one if you had an unhappy childhood or your family life is bad.

Red Goldstone

Red/orange and sparkling with tiny stars, *the* magick crystal for being out there and up there with the winners.

• good luck if you are entering competitions or raffles • to find your way if you are always getting lost in new places •

- Seven small goldstones in a charm bag if there is a lot of competition for what you are applying for or trying out for.
- A single one boosts confidence with people you don't know or with a big group.

Blue Goldstone

Deep blue with sparkly stars.

• for all performances • keep with you when you are doing astrology or astronomy • helps you to get good profiles, references, and qualifications • use if you want to travel, especially overseas •

- Seven small ones in a charm bag with your dearest wish written and put inside the bag.
- Use a single one to overcome fear of the dark, of flying, or of staying away from home overnight.

Sunstone

Golden-orange with a sparkly iridescent sheen.

• for overcoming cliques • to bring travel chances and adventures • opens doors to opportunities to shine and lead • brings good luck in your driving test, examinations, and any moneymaking schemes • drives away spooks •

- Five small ones carried in a charm bag to create laughter and fun.
- Use a single one when starting new sports, especially extreme ones, or to make friends at the gym.

Unakite

Salmon pink and olive green, mixed.

• to stop panic • for true and lasting love • good if you have trouble finding things • brings luck when you must take a risk for success but fear you will fail (you won't) •

- Three in a charm bag carried to soothe any food issues and worries about your appearance.
- Use a single one if you have a mountain of chores and homework/assignments/revision to finish and not enough time.

USEFUL CHARM BAG MIXES

You can also, as well as using three or more of the same crystals, mix your crystals to get exactly the right ingredients for your charm bag purpose. The combinations below are some that work really well.

For any competition.

Use two aventurine and one amazonite in a green bag.

For meeting a new love or keeping an existing love going.

Use two matching rose quartz hearts plus one unakite in a pink bag.

For protection from bullies.

Use a bloodstone, an ametrine, and a tiger's-eye in a brown or gray bag.

For success at school or work.

Use a turquoise or lapis lazuli, a citrine, and a unakite in a blue bag.

For travel and safety.

Use an amazonite, a chrysocolla, and a turquoise in a silver or blue bag.

To stop online bullying.

Use a malachite, a dendritic agate, and a turquoise or chrysocolla in a red bag.

To make you shine in every way.

Use a sunstone, a blue goldstone, and an orange goldstone in a gold bag.

To draw to you whatever you want.

Use two magnetized hematite crystals and a sunstone in a gold bag.

To curb anixety and depression or if you are afraid of ghosts.

Use a smoky quartz, an angelite, and a purple fluorite in a purple bag.

To bring you money.

Use a golden tiger's-eye, an orange goldstone, and a citrine in a brown bag.

For wishes, luck, and happiness in every part of your life.

Use one of your zodiac crystals, a clear quartz, and an amethyst in a white bag.

HOW TO MAKE A CRYSTAL CHARM BAG POWERFUL

There are one or two extra things to add to your collection so you can cast a spell to fill your charm bag with power that will last as long as needed.

SETTING UP YOUR CRYSTAL ALTAR

For doing spells imagine your crystal table, whether it is round or square, with a clock face flat on it.

Picture the four main times: 12 o'clock is farthest away from you, then we go down to 3 o'clock for our second quarter on the right, then to 6 o'clock directly in front of you as you face the table, then the 9 o'clock quarter on the left taking us back to 12.

THE SETUP:

At your 12 o'clock put a small bowl of salt, which stands for the Earth. This is the place we start the spell. *At your 3 o'clock* leave your incense stick in any flower fragrance in a holder. This is for the Air that gets the spell stirring. In the center of the table, instead of the usual white candle, have a small dish to hold the bag of chosen crystals you will be filling with magickal power. You can carry this bag with you afterward.

Now you will take your white candle that is usually in the middle of your crystal altar (white stands for just about everything) down to your *6 o'clock* directly in front of you as you face the table. This is for Fire, the fuel and power that lifts the magick. Put here also your crystal wand or pointed clear quartz we used earlier for filling your crystals with power.

The bowl of water stays exactly where it is in the *9 o'clock position* for the Water that mixes everything together in the spell. The crystals you keep in your special crystal altar can stay exactly where they are.

CREATING YOUR CRYSTAL SPELL

Before you begin doing magick, touch the center of your brow where your psychic third eye is. Ask that only goodness and light will enter. You can ask your angels and guardians to protect you if you wish.

STAGE 1: THE INTENT

Take your time to decide what exactly you are making the charm bag for. Remember that it can attract whatever or whomever you want or protect you against whomever or whatever you don't want in your life. Don't forget that **under the rules of magick, you can harm no one**, no matter how horrid they are. But you can use magick to stop their bad behavior from reaching you.

STAGE 2: THE CRYSTALS

As I said earlier, you can have in your magick charm bag three, five, seven, nine, or thirteen crystals. On the whole, three is plenty.

If you really can't work out which crystal is best and don't have time to check the lists of crystals, put your hands in your rainbow crystal bowl. Without looking, pick the number of crystals you want. Hold them in your open-cupped hands. Say what you want them to do and put them one by one in the charm bag. It always works.

Place your bag or pouch in the central dish.

STAGE 3: STARTING THE MAGICK

1. Light the candle at the 6 o'clock position, and the incense stick at the 3 o'clock position from the candle. Say as you light each, *"I ask for (say what you are asking for)."* At this point, name the spell wish the bag is being created for.

2. Lift up the central dish containing the bag of chosen crystals toward the central candle and say again what you are wishing for.

STAGE 4: THE ENERGIES

Go to 12 o'clock.

1. Take the salt dish in your non-writing hand and sprinkle three circles of salt clockwise around the dish in the center. As you do so, say the spell wish words three times. Return the salt to its place.

2. Take the incense stick out of its holder. Holding it like a pen, draw smoke spirals clockwise all around the charm bag on the dish three times. Again say your chosen words three times. Return the incense stick to its holder.

3. Pass the symbol dish clockwise three times carefully around the white candle. Say the same words three times as you do so. Return the dish containing the bag of chosen crystals to the center.

4. Holding the water dish in your non-writing hand, sprinkle three clockwise circles of water droplets around the symbol dish. Say the same words three times. Return the bowl to its place.

STAGE 5: INCREASING THE POWER

1. Hold your crystal wand in your writing hand, circling it clockwise, facing your crystal place. Move it faster and faster.
2. Say your spell bag wish faster and faster. Make your spell wish only four or five words so it is easier to chant.
3. Continue moving the wand and speaking even faster until you feel that the power of the spell has reached its height.

STAGE 6: RELEASING THE POWER

1. When you feel the moment is right, start to move the wand or your hands slower and slower. As you do so, speak quieter and quieter until you are just whispering.
2. When your words can't be heard anymore, press your wand gently into the charm bag. Say, *"Power/protection enter with me that I may take the power of the spell with me."*

STAGE 7: ENDING THE SPELL

1. Hold the charm bag, blow out the candles, and thank your guardians.

2. Press down hard with your feet, fingers pointing downward. This will bring you back to the everyday world. Then tidy your crystal altar.

3. Keep the charm bag with you or in a bedside drawer. You can touch it any time you need to feel the power or protection of the spell in the days ahead.

A CRYSTAL SPELL BAG PARTY

It is great fun to hold a spell bag party, especially on the crescent or full moon, as both are good times for wish magick.

Group Crystal Readings

You can start with readings for one another at your crystal party.

1. Sit in a circle. Pass the rainbow bowl of crystals or a bowl containing your fifteen basic stones around the circle. The first person (you) asks a question and picks a crystal without looking, then puts the bowl on the floor. Hand the chosen crystal to the person on the right.

2. Even if no one knows the meanings of the crystals, the person now holding the chosen crystal says, without thinking, what s/he feels from the crystal vibes to answer the question. Keep it going quickly.

3. The person who answers the question puts the crystal back in the bowl, asks a question, and shuts their eyes to pick a new crystal from the bowl.

4. The person to their right holds that crystal and gives a quick answer.

5. This continues until everyone has asked and answered a question.

Charm Bag Party

Another fun activity to do at your party is making charm bags. Use the method below, or modify to suit the needs of your guests.

1. Have a selection of small crystals in a big bowl and ask everyone to pick three without looking.
2. Have a selection of white bags, one for each person to put their crystals in.
3. Ask each person to decide what they are making their bag for.
4. Make a mini altar on a big heatproof tray in the middle of the room with salt at 12 o'clock, an incense stick at 3 o'clock, a white candle at 6 o'clock, and a bowl of water at 9 o'clock.
5. Put a big dish to hold everyone's bags in the center of the tray.
6. Have everyone sit in a circle around the bags.
7. Explain the spell and choose different people to light the candle and pass the spell bag dish around it during the spell.
8. Make printouts of the spell stages and the words everyone will say.
9. You can sit in the center during the spell to make sure everything happens as it should and to lead the words.
10. Invite people at the right time during the spell to perform their actions.
11. Have a dress rehearsal if you want before the actual spell.
12. (Optional)Everyone can say at the same time during the spell, led by you instead of making separate wishes aloud, *"May my wish be granted."*

13. Clap and say over and over again, *"Power of the magick, power of the spell, power of the magick, use the magick well."* As before, say it faster and faster then slower and slower.
14. Instead of touching the bags at the end everyone can point their two hands, fingers together, toward the bags to release the magic.

CHAPTER 9

CRYSTALS AND DREAMS

Crystals are very useful at night if you can't get to sleep or you have nightmares. They can protect you if you're scared of the dark (a lot of people of all ages are). Sometimes you can feel spooked by ghosts, especially if friends on a sleepover have been messing with questionable spells from the internet. Perhaps you were all playing with Ouija boards and you can sense spirits who haven't gone away. But crystals will soon have your room and dreams peaceful again.

Crystals will also help you to have peaceful sleep when you're really tired and toss and turn all night. They can also bring special dreams where you can travel in sleep wherever you want, to other lands if you wish. You might want to visit someone who lives in another state. You might even want to explore past lives you have occasionally seen when you have been daydreaming. This is called astral traveling, and I will explain how you can do this later in the chapter.

Dreams of past lives or traveling to other lands in your sleep just happen, but wouldn't it be great if you could make the right dreams appear whenever you wish? You can by using dream crystals.

You may want to have a special place in your journal for recording your dreams and any answers you get from them.

SLEEP AND DREAM CRYSTALS

Some crystals are especially good for peaceful sleep, others for keeping away nightmares and for creating the kind of dreams you want when you want them. But any dream crystal can be used for absolutely anything to do with sleep and dreams. It's ok if you've only got one or two of the crystals I mention. The asterisks (*) mark new crystals.

Most of the dream crystals that appear in this chapter have been covered before. Some you will have in your basic fifteen crystals or your ever-growing bowl of crystals. For those I will just describe their dream use. For new ones like iodalite and blue celestine, you can check in the Treasury of Crystals on PAGES 129–134 for other good things these crystals will do in your daily life.

Put the dream crystals you collect in a little bowl by your bed. Sometimes, pick one with your eyes closed before sleep to see which crystal is best to protect you during the night. Hold the chosen crystal and say, if you're not asking for a special kind of dream such as love or traveling, *"May I sleep safe all night, have beautiful dreams, and wake happy in the morning."*

Put the crystal next to the bed and close your eyes, imagining the crystal light all around you.

Amethyst

• relaxes you if you have had a bad day or a fight before bed • keep under your pillow to prevent insomnia and nightmares and to bring beautiful dreams • keep beneath the bed of an old or sick pet to bring peaceful sleep • shielding if you have lots of technology in your bedroom •

Celestine

Pale to medium blue, also white, looks like ice crystals.

• slows you down after a crazy day • settles you if you are sleeping somewhere you don't know well or don't feel welcome • keep by the bed if you wake in the night panicking • for past life and extraterrestrial dreams • for seeing angels and guardians • for going to beautiful unknown places in your dreams •

Fluorite

• dreams of past ancient lives • dreams of magickal creatures such as unicorns, parrots, and butterflies; underwater lands; and the fairy people • sleeping peacefully if you aren't well or if you are totally stressed out about the coming day •

Howlite

Dyed sky blue, sometimes with veins. You have already learned about white howlite, but the blue version seems to work better for dream work.

• all-purpose • brings peaceful sleep and happy dreams • helps you to know you are dreaming and so can control the dream • for dreams of angels and spirit guardians, extraterrestrials, and your power animals •

Mangano or pink calcite

• protects against bad ghosts at night • links you with your guardian angels, fairies, and nature spirits in dreams • for finding your past-life love • for beautiful dreams of present or future love • makes you wake feeling beautiful and loved •

Moonstone

• protects you against nightmares • to overcome insomnia • for astral travel • for dreams of love, especially around the full moon • prevents harm from the paranormal world entering your dreams while you are dream-traveling •

Pearl

• to balance mood swings, hormonal or caused by problems in your life • helps you to relax and not toss and turn all night • brings beautiful dreams, especially of water, magickal sea creatures like mermaids, and the ocean •

Rose quartz

• helps you to sleep if you have been hurt or teased during the day • soothing if you are feeling lonely or unloved when you go to bed • to bring dreams of love • for gentle undisturbed sleep •

Rutilated quartz

• for past life dreams • for traveling in sleep and meeting nature spirits • a crystal form of the dream catcher to capture bad dreams inside the crystal before they reach you • brings answers in dreams •

Selenite

• stops you from having dreams about future disasters if you are very psychic • protective if you fear the dark or don't feel safe where you are sleeping • comforting if you are missing your mother, grandmother, or sister • takes you to other realms and safely home • brings you dreams of angels, gods and goddesses, and magickal creatures •

LUCID DREAMING USING CRYSTALS

To be able to travel wherever you want in dreams, often called astral travel, is not scary. You don't physically leave your body, so you can't get stuck. It is the psychic part of your mind that opens up endless possibilities in sleep. You are always in control, so nothing bad can happen.

But how? Just by *knowing* you are dreaming, which is called lucid dreaming. It's easier than you might think. Here's how:

Discovering in sleep that you are dreaming

Just follow the steps below. It might take a few tries, but if you're patient it is a fabulous feeling and power to have.

Just before sleep, light your bedside lamp. Don't use a candle; they are dangerous when you are falling asleep. Hold your chosen dream crystal toward the lamp beam as you lie propped up in bed, and say, *"When I see this crystal in my dream, I will know that I am dreaming. Then I will know I can go anywhere, do anything, and end the dream when I am ready."* Close your eyes and, still holding your crystal, see it in your mind's eye getting larger and larger. Repeat the words five or six times.

Then open your eyes and look at the crystal. Now close your eyes again and picture the crystal in your mind. Repeat these actions alternately for two or three minutes. When you are ready, drift into sleep after putting your crystal next to your bed.

As you close your eyes, picture the crystal in your mind and imagine the crystal all around you. Picture a doorway of light leading to the stars and you are floating or flying through them. Keep saying the words softer and softer and slower and slower until you fall asleep.

The first night you try, you may find that you don't remember you are dreaming. But you may find yourself holding the crystal as you wake. If not, pick it up, look into it, and say aloud as much of any dream you can remember. Do this every night, and each morning you will remember more and more of your dreams, even if you usually don't. If you wake in the night, hold your crystal for a minute and say the words again. Picture the doorway and the stars.

After a few nights, or maybe longer, you will have that wonderful dream moment. Even if you can't see the crystal in your dreams, you will *know* it is a dream. This means you can change anything, do anything, or go anywhere in the dream, and you can zap nightmares right out of existence. If you don't like the way a dream is going, change the ending so you are the hero and you will wake ready for anything and everyone. In the morning, your power-filled vibes will just flow out of you and everyone will assume you've had a major makeover. You have supercharged yourself with *dream power*.

FINDING LOVE IN DREAMS

For hundreds of years, maybe longer, people have used dreams to discover a future lover or to call a love that is right for them.

Of course, love dreams often come unplanned, but whatever age you are and whatever your future plans are, it can be fun to dream of your future love. Sometimes you find that person from the dream in the weeks afterward. You may meet seemingly by chance at an event you don't usually go to or at a boring family party where a cousin drags along a friend. It might be someone you *do* know, for example, the guy or girl who fixed your computer when it crashed. Then you know it is meant to be.

HOW TO DREAM OF LOVE

This is a personal dream love ritual based on folk rituals from old European traditions. It is good for finding a special person in the future.

THE RITUAL

1. Before bed, put on a small bedside light so it shines onto your crystal. Hold your dream crystal in your non-writing hand as you sit up in bed.
2. Brush your hair one hundred times with your writing hand. Keep holding your crystal and look into it through half-closed eyes as you brush.
3. While brushing, say over and over very softly, *"In my dreams come to me, a love so true, that I may see. Come to me in sleep that we may walk together in our dreams. Then I do entreat, that in the light of day, if and when right to be, we soon shall meet."* Put down the brush and turn off the light.
4. Lie in bed with your eyes closed, still holding your crystal. Whisper into it over and over till you are nearly asleep, *"Come to me in sleep that we may walk together in our dreams."* Put your crystal by the bedside and drift into sleep.
5. Hold your crystal before getting up in the morning and replay your dream for clues as to where and how you will meet.
6. If the dream didn't come, be patient and it will happen in the weeks ahead.

FINDING ANSWERS IN DREAMS

Crystal dreams can also answer all kinds of questions, even about the future. The more you work with crystals, the more psychic you become. People have asked dream questions since ancient times. Below you'll find one method for getting the answers you need.

1. Write a question on a piece of paper.
2. Once you are in bed, read it aloud nine times.
3. Fold it small and put it on your bedside table with your chosen dream crystal on top. Rutilated quartz is the very best for answering dream questions.
4. When you wake, before getting out of bed write down everything with a blue or green pen you can remember about the dream, then make it into a story. The answer should become instantly clear. Sometimes a dream will warn you of hidden facts about people or a situation you were asking about. This may be proven true very soon, and you can avoid trouble by being prepared. Dreams can jump us ahead timewise. They also alert us to things our natural psychic radar picked up that our daytime logical mind did not.

Dreams are full of symbols, so, you may need to work out what the pictures and story mean.

If you asked what you were doing at work that made everyone hate you, a dream of being caught in the snow might tell you that you really *were* being frozen out at your new internship by spiteful people. They are jealous because you are doing so well, though the ringleaders said it was *you* being unfriendly.

See who rescues you. It may be someone at work who is sympathetic and will help, or your trainer/boss/mentor if you confide in them. Maybe you dig your own way out and ski off to a better apprenticeship, while the envious crowd are all still stuck in the snow. On the other hand, it could be your work is going to be recognized as the best by the boss (the rescuer?) and you get put on a special fast-track course.

PAST-LIFE CRYSTAL DREAMS

You may already have experienced past-life travel to other times and places in your dreams. Sometimes these past-life dreams just happen. Perhaps you asked in your dream work to go back to the past. Either way, some of the people you have met in your dreams may have looked awfully familiar. Some you were pleased to see, others less so.

Past-life dreams, whether they just come or you call them, seem very real, and you may think about them all day. It may be that in your present life you have wanted since you were small to, for example, know all about ancient Egypt. If so, this would be a good place to start planning a past-life dream. Young children up to about seven years old often actually remember past lives, and then those past lives will fade and only come back in dreams.

You may in this life meet someone and instantly feel you know them well. They may feel the same affinity with you. You may have a particular fear you can't explain of being trapped in an elevator until you have a dream where you are shut in a dungeon. Because you know how to change dreams by knowing you are dreaming, you can let yourself out of that dungeon and, amazingly, the fear goes away.

But past-life dreaming doesn't work for everyone right away. If it isn't working for you after trying a few times, try instead the crystal pathway to past lives while you're awake. Your past-life crystals will take you there, one way or the other, when the time is right.

GATEWAY CRYSTALS

In myth and movies, other worlds and other dimensions are reached through gateways and magickal doorways. Gazing into your dream crystals, you may see or sense a doorway inside a crystal.

The dream crystals that are good for past lives that you have already learned about are:

• Celestine • Fluorite • Mangano calcite • Opalite • Rutilated quartz •

You can also use the following for your past-life dreams:

- A **CRYSTAL GEODE CAVE**, made of tiny **AMETHYSTS** or **CITRINE**, still in the rock.
- An **AGATE GEODE**, an agate with lots of tiny crystals in the center.
- An **AGATE SLICE**, often dyed. This is a thin piece of agate you can see light through.
- A small **CELESTINE** crystal sphere with holes in the center that looks as if something took a bite out of it, making natural doorways.
- Any see-through crystals like **CLEAR QUARTZ** with lots of markings inside have lots of gateways. You can use a crystal ball or sphere.
- Squat pyramids, a shape that brings out psychic powers in clear quartz, amethyst, or **SMOKY QUARTZ**.

Agates and celestines are cheap, and you only need one about the size of a very small orange. Your geodes can be small as long as they are like a mini cave and are just as good for past worlds as gigantic geode caves.

CRYSTAL GATEWAYS TO THE PAST IN YOUR SLEEP

For safety, you should use a battery-powered candle by your bed. You can use these for any dream work to create a flickering doorway of light to shine on your crystal.

Before going to sleep, ask to see a particular past life you feel connected to or say, *"Whatever I most need to see tonight."*

You can also ask a question, for example, "Why is my big sister so mean to me?"

You may well see her hundreds of years ago, jealous and scowling in her ugly wedding dress because your folks in that life married her off to a rich old man to save the family fortunes while you ran away with the gorgeous young musician she really liked. You can try harder in this life to give her a break even when she is horrid. But as a result of knowing you are experiencing a past world, you can help your sister in that life to put those feelings behind her and find happiness. Maybe you could change the ending to the two of you going off together and joining another group of musicians. As a bonus of changing that past-life ending, you will also come out of the dream with *don't mess with me, it wasn't my fault* vibes in your waking world. She may sense this when she goes too far.

Sometimes you may wake before you get the chance to change the ending of a past-life dream, or, for that matter, any dream, for the better. In that case, lie in bed and go back to where the dream stopped. If you can't get back into the dream, tell the story in your mind or out loud with a new ending. It works!

STAGE 1: GOING THROUGH THE DREAM GATEWAY

1. Light your battery candle next to your bed.
2. Put a few drops of lavender or chamomile fragrance under your pillow (not on top of your pillow because it could get in your eyes and sting).
3. If you prefer, treat yourself to a sleep pillow (a pillow filled with chamomile and lavender).

4. Have as background music natural sounds such as the sea or birds. These are sounds that existed in all times and so can carry you back to old lives.
5. Work in total darkness except for the light of the battery candle.
6. If you can't see a gateway in your crystal, focus on one of the holes in it to make the doorway. You can also shine the light on to the surface and imagine a doorway of light.
7. Ask your spirit guardians to be with you. If you see something that frightens you in that old world, they will stay with you while you change the ending to something happy and free. After you wake, you will know you will never have that fear again.
8. For any pointed crystal, like a pyramid, or a rough unpolished crystal, like a geode with tiny crystals, hold it to the light in your non-writing hand. Gently stroke the crystal with your writing hand for a minute or two from the base to the tip and down again to the base and up again to create a rhythmic movement.
9. If you are using one of your smooth tumblestone dream crystals you used in the previous chapter, hold it in the hand you do not write with. With the index finger of your writing hand make circles all over on the crystal surface until you connect with it. Now cup the dream tumblestone in your open hands.
10. Look into the crystal or hold it so light is on the surface and see or imagine your doorway.

STAGE 2: MOVING THROUGH THE CRYSTAL INTO THE PAST LIFE

1. Close your eyes. Breathe gently, in and out.
2. Count from your present age down to one slowly aloud, picturing in your mind the doorway getting larger.
3. Close your eyes and see the doorway in your mind.
4. Walk through it. Start to see your past life and what is around you as you drift into sleep.

CHAPTER 10
CRYSTALS AND PSYCHIC POWERS

USING A CRYSTAL BALL

Every fortune-teller needs a crystal ball. Clear quartz balls or spheres are the best for reading. You can use a small, clear quartz mini crystal ball, totally round, as long as it has plenty of markings inside if you're not ready to buy a larger, more expensive one.

Even with a full-size crystal ball, you don't really want one much larger than what will sit in the palm of your writing hand (think medium-size orange). That makes it easy to turn it around with the other hand to catch the light and look for the pictures inside.

Choose one with plenty of markings (known as *inclusions*) and clear areas inside. When you look inside, you can see the shapes of stars, animals, birds, trees, and full scenes. Each time you look into the ball and ask a different question, you will see different pictures.

GETTING TO KNOW YOUR CRYSTAL BALL

If you do get to choose your own ball, go to a crystal store or new age shop and hold different ones until one feels just right. If not, hold your hand a few inches in front of your tablet or computer at an online store that is selling them, enlarge each one, and feel your fingertips tingle when you have found the right one. But if you are given one, you can make it your own as you use it.

Before crystal-ball reading for the first time, and every time you use it, gently polish it with a soft white cloth. Then ask for the blessing of the guardian of the crystal (even the smallest crystal ball will have its own guardian who keeps you safe while you work).

After the reading, thank your guardian and say, *"Until we meet again."* In any psychic or magick work it is important to return to the everyday world. Blow softly three times on the ball, repolish it, and return it to your crystal place.

Record in your crystal journal every picture you see while crystal-ball reading and what it means to you.

HOW TO READ YOUR CRYSTAL BALL

1. The first time you use it, turn and twist the ball in all directions between your hands. Look into it and see how many **PICTURES**, made of the lines inside and the spaces between them, you can see in the ball. At this stage don't ask any questions. Write or draw the pictures afterward and decide what they mean to you. In time, words will come into your mind to tell you what it means.
2. **INITIALS** within the sphere refer to people you know. If you see a number of letters in the ball, write them down and they will form or almost form whole words when rearranged.
3. **NUMBERS** will give you a time frame, whether weeks, months, or years if you are working for a college degree, or

a sport, creative, or career plan. You will know which time frame fits.

4. If you see an **ANIMAL** or **BIRD**, ask is it fierce like a lion or gentle like a pet? If a bird, is it flying and soaring with huge wings, perhaps hunting? Is it a bird in a cage? If so, does it want to be free? Apply these to people and situations in your life.

If you can't see anything in the ball, close your eyes slowly. Open them slowly and blink. Look into the ball again and name aloud what you think or sense you *see* without thinking. The trick is to be really fast before logic tells you it's all a load of rubbish.

If it's still not working, close your eyes and imagine the crystal ball getting larger and larger in your mind and let the image appear. This is also good if you need more background details.

SETTING THE SCENE

Work with your crystal ball outdoors if the light is good in sunshine or full moonlight, or indoors by candlelight after dark. If outdoors, work near sweet-smelling flowers or greenery. If indoors, burn frankincense, myrrh, or sandalwood, or a floral, either as an incense stick or an oil-burner fragrance. If you prefer, have a dish of scented potpourri or flowers on the table. Fragrance helps to open your psychic channels even faster.

THE THREE PICTURES METHOD

Now you are ready to ask questions for yourself and, when you feel ready, for other people.

1. Begin by placing and curving your non-writing hand underneath the ball and your writing hand curved above it. This creates the psychic link between you and the crystal

ball. If you are reading for someone else, ask them to put both their hands cupped over the top of the ball.

2. Place your hands on top of theirs for a minute or two.
3. Take the ball from them and hold it again, non-writng hand underneath and the other on top. This is a good time to ask your question or let the person you are reading for ask a question.
4. Gaze into the ball to find your first picture. Start in the center and work outward as you hold it lightly in your non-writing hand. You can at this point rest it on a table or on your crystal altar if you want.
5. Say aloud what you see in the crystal ball and any words you hear inside your head. Explain what you feel about the image you are seeing. Do you feel happy, sad, scared, worried? Look at what is around your picture and what is happening.
6. Record what you say or scribble down your own pictures and words as you go. Don't think logically, just talk until you run out of ideas.
7. If you are reading for a friend or family member, show them the first picture in the ball. Trace the outline on the surface and ask them what they feel that picture means to them. Put their ideas together with yours.
8. Pass your hands over the ball in counterclockwise circles to clear it. Blow softly on the ball three times and look for the second picture. See how it develops the ideas of the first picture and adds to the message. Again, if reading for someone else, ask them about the picture.

9. Do the same for the third picture. If reading for someone else, ask them again, and you will see how you have built up an answer.

PAST, PRESENT, AND FUTURE

As you practice more you can, if you wish, use the first crystal-ball picture to tell you what has already happened. The second will reveal what you need to know right now in the present to help you to know what to do and how to act. The third question tells you what will happen if you follow the advice of the second picture.

Exploring past lives with friends

You can do this if you are having friends over for a sleepover or a crystal party. Discovering if you shared past lives makes for a fun activity.

1. Light white candles around the room and a single larger white one in the center of the room.
2. Draw the curtains and light floral incense sticks.
3. Sit in a circle on cushions around the middle white candle.
4. You only need one crystal ball or pyramid.
5. Ask the guardians to keep you safe as you travel together.
6. Count aloud slowly from twenty down to one, holding the ball or pyramid yourself first.
7. Holding the ball, focus on the candle in the center of the circle. Say, *"I ask to see when we were all together in a previous life."*
8. Still holding the ball, gaze into it. Describe what you see, hear, and feel. Just let the words come. Don't think logically

or try to second-guess yourself. You may see a whole scene of some previous life in the ball.

9. Pass the ball clockwise. The next person says the same words as they look at the central candle.Then they look into the ball and add what they can see in it.
10. Bit by bit, as everyone says and does the same, you may be building up an old world where you were all together.
11. When all have finished speaking, go around the circle again, each person saying what gift they want to bring back to this present life from that past world you shared.
12. Go around once more. Each person now names any fears or worries they want to leave in that old world.
13. Put the ball in the center in front of the candle so light shines on it. Talk about what you all see in the ball and candlelight. Just call out.
14. When you sense there is no more, count back, this time slowly from one up to twenty. Thank the guardians and angels for protecting you and say, *"Until we meet again."*

You will have much to talk about. You may also have some interesting dreams if you are having a sleepover.

USING A CRYSTAL PENDULUM

By now, you are no longer apprentice crystal seers but rapidly becoming crystal experts, regardless of how many crystals you own.

Another psychic art to learn is using a crystal pendulum for fortune-telling. Pendulums are also incredibly useful for deciding between choices.

Though there are different kinds of pendulums, crystal pendulums are the best as crystals are millions of years old, so they're pretty wise.

A clear quartz pendulum—a pointed crystal on a chain—works really well. You might prefer hematite, jade, rose quartz, or amethyst. Most pendulums are long and cylinder shaped, with a pointed end. Some are a diamond shape, ending in a sharp point. You can also use a favorite crystal pendant, with the chain or cord twisted to make a single chain.

TUNING IN YOUR PENDULUM

You can get over the tricky problem of trying to work out which swing means *yes* and which swing means *no* by training your pendulum just as you would a new puppy.

1. Hold your pendulum loosely in your writing hand.
2. Wrap enough chain around your index and middle finger so the chain is long enough to swing freely. You don't want it long enough to drag on the surface of or a table. Experiment until it feels right.
3. Swing it deliberately a few times slowly clockwise, or whatever movement you want to be *yes*. Say, *"Let that be yes."*
4. Swing it deliberately a few times slowly counterclockwise, or whatever you want to be *no* (choose an opposite direction or movement to *yes*). Say, *"Let that be no."*
5. The stronger the swing *yes* or *no* when you ask your pendulum a question, the more definite the answer is. If the crystal pendulum doesn't move or makes a crazy alternate yes and no response, you may need to ask the question in a different way. It can only answer yes or no; it cannot choose between options.
6. Before beginning any crystal pendulum work, plunge your crystal pendulum in and out of a glass of water nine times to clean it of energy.

7. Ask that your pendulum always tell you the truth. Ask also that while you work you will be protected from all harm and danger from the spirit world.
8. Wipe it dry with a soft cloth you keep just for your pendulum.

Asking single questions

For everyday issues, a single question will usually provide you with the answer if the matter's not clear. It also helps if friends and family are pushing you in different directions. You can ask detailed questions such as, "Should I take a weekend and evening job so I can save for my first car, even though I have a lot of homework to do?"

The pendulum will tell you what you *need* to hear, using information that your psychic radar picks up that we may miss.

Record the question and answer and any ideas that came into your head about the answer in a special section of your journal.

Asking more than one question

Sometimes you need a bit more information or the answer isn't clear. Here are two options to try when that is the case.

OPTION 1:

After you use your pendulum, swap it to your non-writing hand and, using a piece of white paper and a blue or green pen (any sort), start to write.

First write the question you asked and then underneath it let your hand write. Do not think about what you're writing, just write.

Play soft music if it helps you to relax. If you want, ask your favorite angel or guardian to help, or the beautiful, shimmering Archangel Metatron, who is the angel of writing. If you prefer, just let your psychic radar show the signals it has picked up in the words you write without thinking. When you feel the pen slowing, put it down and read what you have written.

OPTION 2:

After the pendulum has answered the first question, let more questions come into your mind, one at a time.

Keep a chart of questions and answers in your crystal journal so you can work out afterward what is happening (see the example below and on PAGE 94).

Write your first question at the top of the page and whether you got a weak or strong *yes* or *no*.

Clear your mind after each question, imagining a teacher wiping a whiteboard clean after a lesson. The questions your psychic mind gives you may seem odd, but they are ones we need to ask.

Write the second question, allowing it to appear in your mind. This time hold the pendulum in the air a few inches above the question. Watch how strongly the crystal moves. Take your time.

Keep recording and continue asking questions until you have your answer.

Example:

Sam's parents and grandparents have all been physicians. His parents are urging him to choose the right courses for his future admission to medical school.

But Sam loves cooking and works weekends and vacations in his best friend's parents' restaurant. The head chef has spotted his talent and says he could, with training, work for a top restaurant. Sam wants to enroll in culinary school at seventeen and get a degree in culinary arts.

Sam's first answer shows he doesn't want to upset his family, but by his last question his smart psychic radar has offered a solution.

QUESTION	YES	NO
Should I train as a doctor?		Weak
Should I allow my family to influence my career choice?		Strong
Will it be easy to persuade them to let me train as a chef?		Strong
Can my friend's parents help?	Strong	
Should I invite my parents to the restaurant on a quiet night and ask the chef to let me prepare the meal?	Strong	
If I persist can I become a chef?	Strong	

Sam's family was impressed after talking to the restaurant owners, and even more so when Sam prepared them a wonderful and very professional meal. They have promised to support him.

Choosing between different options

If you have several different choices and you can't decide, write down your choices, as many as you like, on separate small squares of paper, turn them blank-side up, mix them up, and put them in a circle.

Pass your pendulum clockwise slowly over each one, a few inches in the air above them. You may instantly feel a downward pull over one square. See if the pendulum will continue. There may be a second choice with a less strong reaction, or you may need to combine two choices. Alternatively, over the right choice you may feel a strong tingling in the hand or fingers in which you are holding the pendulum. If no choice has been made, perhaps there is another choice you need to add.

Finding lost objects

You have five minutes to catch the bus, and you can't find your assignment, your bus pass, or your wallet.

Stop; pick up your pendulum. Plunge it once into a glass of water, shake it, and go back to the very last time you had the missing item. Your mom was coming through the door at the same minute and asked you to help carry the groceries, and you had the item in your hand.

Holding your pendulum, ask, "Please take me to— " and start walking. The pendulum will swing in its *yes* response while you are on track and continue to swing faster the closer it gets to the missing item.

If it stops, stop too and turn slowly in all directions. Try each direction. If the pendulum makes the *no* response, you're off track.

Return to where the pendulum stopped. Try another direction until it goes into *yes* mode. You may, as you get closer, feel a tingling in your fingers as well as a faster, stronger swing.

If the swing slows, stops, or goes into *no* mode, go back to the place of greatest activity.

The missing object will be under something close, maybe a laundry pile or a piece of furniture. Search, and you might just make that bus!

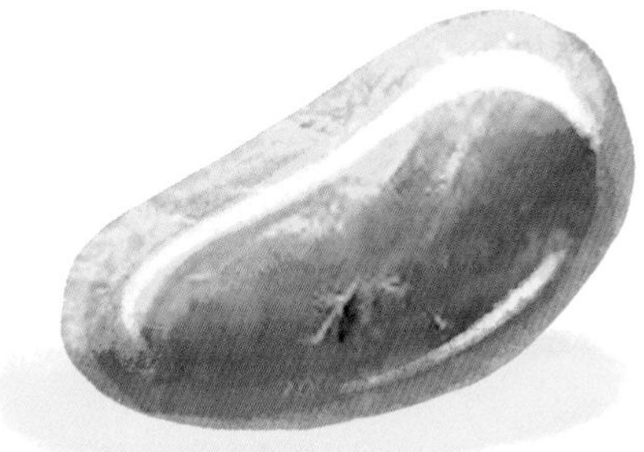

CHAPTER 11

* HEALING WITH CRYSTALS *

We all have the power to heal. When we offer a hug to a crying friend, we are giving healing energy because all healing is based on love and care. Crystals make our natural healing powers a hundred times more powerful. If we trust our crystals and hold them loosely, they will guide us as to how to hold or move them in every situation. Crystals can also be used for sending healing energies to your pets, people you know, and places where there has been a disaster, even if you are far away.

When you were young, your mom could make you feel better when you fell by rubbing your scraped knee. She can still make you feel better with a hug when your heart is broken. Even your cranky pet relaxes when you stroke her. Crystals are like one big psychic hug.

Of course, if you are ill the first port of call is always the doctor, and if your pet is unwell, the veterinarian.

CRYSTAL CALM

You may be stressed, perhaps before a visit to the dentist. You might be going to the doctor for a shot. It could be a major exam worrying you, or that you know you are going to see someone who teases you. Here is a quick way to use crystals to find your calm:

1. Go somewhere you can be alone, even the bathroom.
2. Place a round tumblestone rose quartz, amethyst, or blue lace agate between your open-cupped hands.
3. Slowly hold the crystal close to your face, breathing gently in and out through your nose.
4. On every out breath, imagine dull red or wispy gray anxious energies flowing out. On the *in* breaths, picture the color of the stone flowing inside you and filling you with calm.
5. Keep it in your pocket after you're done, Even if you can't hold the crystal all the time, as long as you are touching it you can picture that calming light flowing through you.

CRYSTAL ENERGY

Crystals are revivers if you need to perform well, need to get some instant oomph, or are getting back into the dating game and are scared.

Touch or hold your citrine or clear quartz. Breathe in its light and breathe out dull brown muddy wisps of doubt.

DISCOVERING YOUR HEALING ENERGIES

There are two kinds of healing. The first is called contact, direct, or touch healing and the second is called absent or distance healing.

Contact or Direct Healing

Because direct crystal healing can take quite a lot of energy out of you, I would suggest you do this for yourself or maybe for a really special friend or two where you can work on one another. If your mom has a headache, you can use it on her. Rose quartz or amethyst dipped in cold water and held gently on the temples are the very best for headaches.

Because we have a two-way bond with our pets (when you are sad your pets always make you feel better just by being there), they are ideal to practice healing on.

The key to successful crystal healing is to relax. Allow the crystals to move in the directions and for the amount of time needed, spontaneously. You can hold them either on the body through clothes or two or three inches away from your own body or that of the friend, family member, or pet you are helping.

Whether healing a person, animal, or place, ask your guardians to help you heal and that the results will be the right ones. Sometimes, if an old pet is really sick, the right healing might be to help them to sleep comfortably and relax in their last months or weeks on earth.

CHOOSING THE RIGHT CRYSTALS FOR CONTACT HEALING

For people, you will need four basic crystals, and for animals, two. You probably have these already. You can use your fifteen fortune-telling or rainbow crystals for healing as long as you wash them under running water before and after. However, you may want to collect a special small set of crystals you keep separate for both contact and distance healing.

If you do have healing crystals, you can keep them in a special bowl lined with a small piece of silk or velvet in any color.

CLEAR QUARTZ: Choose a rounded, smooth stone, small enough to fit in the palm of your hand, or even smaller, the size of a large coin.

Clear quartz will unblock stuck energies that make you feel like you can't be bothered with anything or anyone. It helps too if you always feel tired and cranky. Clear quartz also offers extra stamina if you are struggling to get everything done and are dealing with lots of demands or are unhappy.

Placement: Center of hairline.

CITRINE, a sparking yellow sun crystal that is naturally warming and energizing but is gentler than clear quartz. Wonderful for melting stress and lifting sadness, so you feel quietly confident to go anywhere, do anything, and know everything will turn out exactly as it should.

Placement: Center of upper stomach below the rib cage.

AMETHYST is the best calming crystal if you are anxious, panic easily, or have phobias. It soothes if you are very sensitive to atmospheres or are allergic to lots of different things; hold one on takeoff and landing if you hate flying (also blue sodalite). It will relax you if you have to go to a crowded place; soothes a churning stomach caused by tension.

Placement: Center of the brow above and between the eyes.

ROSE QUARTZ heals hurts of the heart, if you've been let down in love or are having a hard time at home; excellent for easing PMS or menstrual problems; if you have food issues, are teased or bullied, or are naturally shy; good for pregnant pets or those finding mothering difficult and for settling rescue shelter animals.

Placement: On the chest over the heart.

Getting ready for healing

Light a white candle and hold your chosen crystal or crystals between your hands. Say aloud or in your mind what you hope for from the healing.

Hold the crystal first against the center of your hairline, saying,

"From above me the light," then against the center of your brow, saying, "Shines from within me." Hold it next over your heart, saying, "As I offer with love," and finally on your inner sun in the center and bottom of your rib cage, saying, "This crystal healing."

My favorite way of choosing the right crystals for healing directly is to have a bowl of healing crystals (you will need one crystal of each color). Closing your eyes, choose one that feels right. You can also refer to the Treasury of Crystals on **PAGES 129–134**.

Afterward, wash the crystal under running water. If you prefer, spiral the smoke of a floral or tree incense stick over it. Thank the angels, guardians, or whomever you ask for help.

HEALING YOURSELF

ALWAYS CONSULT A PHYSICIAN IF SOMETHING MEDICAL IS WRONG.

1. Pick the crystal that feels right for healing. Choose from your rainbow bowl, your basic fifteen, or use the four suggested healing crystals.
2. Sit quietly and hold the chosen crystal in your open-cupped hands.
3. Name first whatever it is you want to lose. This might be pain, fear, or the symptoms of a migraine or headache coming on. As you hold the crystal, imagine it getting heavier as it is filled with the fear or whatever hurts or upsets you.
4. When it feels too heavy to hold or you sense it is full, wash it under running water. If it is fragile, pass a floral incense stick over it counterclockwise.
5. Place your crystal where light will shine on it.

6. Before going out, pick another crystal and hold it for a minute or two, letting it fill you with strength and calm. Take it with you in a little bag.

CONTACT HEALING OTHERS

For crystal healing you do not need to make contact with the skin. The person you are healing can be fully clothed. However, for close family or friends, you may prefer skin contact on nonintimate parts of the body. But 2–3 inches away is fine.

1. Hold the crystal in your writing hand. Start the healing on the place on your body where that crystal has its natural link with your energies (see **PAGE 98**).
2. Allow the crystal to guide your hand to the place where you or the person you are healing has pain or discomfort. Let the crystal move freely wherever it wants. You may find yourself swaying with the rhythm quite naturally. You can sit or stand. If you are healing someone else they might like to relax lying down.
3. Holding the crystal loosely, allow your crystal to begin moving in ever-widening circles. Trust the crystal.
4. If you totally relax and don't try to control the crystal, you will find that it makes an alternate counterclockwise and clockwise movement. It unblocks the body counterclockwise and then moves clockwise to gently restore health and well-being.

   The crystal may stay circling around where it started or move quite naturally over the whole front of the body. You may find the crystal focuses on your shoulders, small of your back, and knees, as we can carry a lot of stored stress and unhappiness in those body parts. It will do the same on the body of whomever you are healing.

5. If healing your best friend or a family member, you can ask them to turn over halfway through. You may find that what started off as PMS pain from the navel down in fact can be drawing tension from the brow. For yourself, let the crystal circle over the parts of the back you can easily reach.
6. Certain areas may seem to demand extra attention. Your crystal may make soothing movements as it loosens those psychic knots of worry that cause insomnia, or it may circle as you hold it over a tension-knotted brow. Often you may sense these knotted places as jaggedness. If a part of the body doesn't have much energy, the crystal will spiral there for a minute clockwise to top it up.
7. When healing is finished, you will find your crystal circling back to where it began; it will then become perfectly still. Gradually you will sense the body (your own or the person you are healing) vibrating contentedly and you may feel the power fading from the crystal.
8. Wash or pass a flower-scented incense counterclockwise over the crystal.
9. Sit quietly for a while, maybe talking to the person you have healed. If you healed yourself, just relax for a bit.

HEALING PETS

The best crystals to use for healing pets are any brown, gray, or cream banded agate. These will especially soothe an older, chronically sick, or nervous animal.

Jade energizes a pet that is out of sorts and calms a restless animal. You can also put jade regularly in an animal water bowl and leave it overnight before removing the crystal from the water for the pet to drink.

The Ritual:

Before beginning, sit quietly with the animal, stroking and talking gently until s/he settles. When you are ready to begin healing, kneel or sit near the animal or, for a horse, stand about four to six inches away. With your jade or agate, stroke the animal gently and rhythmically. Hold the crystal in your writing hand, following the direction of the fur. Regardless of where the problem is, work first on the legs, the back, and the top of the head, avoiding tender places. Healing will flow through the animal to where it is most needed. Alternatively, you may want to wait until the animal or bird is asleep to heal them. This is especially useful if the pet is cranky or in pain and doesn't want to be touched.

In this case, so as not to wake them, face them about a foot or two away and trace the outline of the animal in the air with the crystal as though your pet was standing or lying directly in front of you. Pass the crystal over the invisible form, feeling in your mind the soft fur or feathers until you get a warm glow in your fingers. Gradually you will sense the crystal energy weakening, and at this point slow down and come to a gentle stop. Sit quietly with the animal for a few minutes. When not in use, wash the crystal and place it underneath the animal bed or near the place the animal rests to continue healing.

REMOTE HEALING WITH CRYSTALS

Crystals can also be used to send healing to a relative in the hospital. You can also direct remote healing to a friend's sick or very old pet even if your friend lives far away. You can even direct your healing to a place you hear about on the news where an earthquake or flood has destroyed whole towns.

If contact crystal healing isn't right for you, try long-distance or remote healing, often called absent healing because the person is not present.

CRYSTALS FOR ABSENT OR DISTANCE HEALING

For energy and dynamic healing use: Clear quartz

Use your clear quartz crystal ball, pyramid, or crystal wand, point outward, held in your writing hand. You could instead cup your hands around a smooth clear quartz.

These will send light, power, and healing through your hands to any person, animal, or place in the world. They will carry hope, strength, and protection to where it is most needed or lift someone who is depressed; it is also good if a friend or family member is having medical tests or difficult treatment, or is in the hospital having an operation.

Clear quartz works particularly well in bright sunlight.

For calm and gentle healing use: Calcite

A large chunk of unpolished calcite in yellow, orange, green, pink, cloudy white, or blue that looks like ice is ideal for slower, gentler healing for people, animals, and places.

Amethyst or rose quartz

Either crystal, as a small sphere or pyramid or a piece of semitransparent or unpolished rose quartz or amethyst.

Calcite, amethyst, and rose quartz are all equally good for bringing new growth and life to places where disasters have caused destruction of homes or wildlife habitats; they will send protection to children in danger in a war zone.

Use any of these three also for overcoming fears, anxiety, panic attacks, and phobias if a friend or family member suffers from these. Above all, they bring peace to wherever and whoever needs it.

These are better in softer light.

SENDING ABSENT OR DISTANCE HEALING

I don't believe you need to ask permission for absent healing, as long as you say before starting, *"May this healing be sent in the way and time that is best for (say person, pet, or place's name here), if and how it is right to receive it."*

You can send healing relief through any of the four crystals I listed above using natural light, sun-, moon-, or candlelight.

Tuesday, the day of Raphael, archangel of healing, and the healing messenger gods like the Roman Mercury or the ancient Greek Hermes, is an especially healing day.

The Ritual:

- Light a white candle after dark for any healing, since white contains all other colors.
- Face the approximate direction of the absent person, animal, or place.
- Hold your crystal up to the light, whether sun-, moon-, or candlelight.

- Now put the healing crystal on your crystal altar. You can set it on any flat surface where you are working if outdoors in full moonlight or bright sunlight.
- Hold your hands downward over the crystal in an inverted cup, not quite touching the crystal. Leave it there until you can feel your fingers tingling, usually after a minute or two. Then take your hands from the crystal.
- With palms horizontal and your index fingers pointing outward, imagine yourself gently pushing beams of colored crystal light toward wherever the person, animal, or place is. If you feel your fingers no longer tingling, put them back over the crystal to take in more light for another minute or two. Then push out again. Bit by bit you will feel the power of your fingers and the crystal slowing down. The healing is now complete.
- You can help an endangered species by sending healing downward. Hold the crystal with your fingers downward in the inverted cup position in the center of a picture of the animals or birds or their habitats.

YOUR HEALING JOURNAL

If you want to make healing a part of your regular crystal work, start a special healing journal. In this you can write the names of people, animals, and places you know or see on television where there is a disaster in need of healing.

Use a book with pages you can take out. Alternatively, obtain a ring binder with loose pages, which makes it easy to add new names and remove names of those who no longer need healing. Some names may always be there. For example, you may worry about children in developing countries.

1. Bless your book by lighting your white healing candle and holding the book closed while between your hands facing the candle. Ask that the Archangel Raphael help in your work, or choose whomever you see as a guardian of light and healing to ask for assistance.
2. Leave the candle burning. Write the names of any people, pets, places, and causes you care about. Note the date of the entry and what kind of healing is needed.
3. Make different sections if you want. Don't worry if you can only think of one or two names to start. Leave space under each name to add any updates in the weeks ahead.
4. Let your candle burn for a few minutes and then blow it out, asking that light be sent to everyone everywhere and/or to places in need of healing.
5. Keep your book closed near your crystal collection when you are not using it. On top of it put either your clear crystal pendulum or your crystal wand, point facing inward to call in healing.

Sending healing through your healing book

You can share your healing book with a special friend or group of friends who are interested in crystal work. You can all add names into the book at any time.

1. Light your white candle and a lavender or rose incense stick, since these are healing scents.

2. Open the book to the first page. Touch each name, whether a person, animal, or place to be healed, with the point of the crystal wand. If you prefer, hold your pendulum over the name, using your writing hand to hold the wand or pendulum. Say for each name, *"May he/she be healed."*
3. If you are working with friends, you can take turns reading the names.
4. When you have finished, blow out the candle and send the light to all who need healing.

Remember, healing should never be a chore. If you don't have time to do this or don't feel like working with the healing book one week, just touch the cover and send a blessing to "all who need healing, known or unknown," before you go to sleep.

APPENDIX A:
READY-MADE MAGICK SPELLS

Here are ten ready-made crystal spells to attract all kinds of good things into your life and to keep or drive away what scares you or makes you unhappy. Copy them into your crystal journal if you want, as they may give you ideas for spells of your own.

Spellcasting can be great fun at a party with a pointed quartz crystal for each person. You can stand in a row or circle depending on the spell and each of you can do a different part of the spell. The Good Fortune spell on PAGE 113, is especially good for parties.

ATTRACTION

You will need

- A pointed clear quartz crystal to act as a wand
- Seven small silver candles, color of the fairy folk, in a row in your special crystal place (set the candles along the base of a mirror you have propped against the wall)

Timing

Monday, which is the day of the moon, or full moon night

The Spell

1. Light the silver candles in front of the mirror so their light shines in it. On full moon night, you may get a bit of moonlight shining in the mirror. Switch off all other lights.
2. Face the mirror, standing behind the candles at a safe distance (no long trailing sleeves with burning candles).
3. Hold the pointed end of your crystal wand toward the mirror in your writing hand.
4. Turn your crystal wand three times clockwise in circles in front of you. It will look as if you are turning it the other way in the mirror.
5. Say, *"This is my wish, I wish I may, I wish I might, have the wish I wish tonight (whisper your wish)."*
6. Then circle your wand three times in the other direction, saying, *"By the power of the fey. Wind and bind enchantment in, bright as moon glow, shimmering gold, fairy magick now unfold."*
7. Blow out the candles fast.

Keep your crystal wand on your bedroom window ledge all night to take in the magick of Monday night or the full moon.

The next day do something, however small, to make your wish come true.

GET OVER LOST LOVE

You will need

- Some yellow children's play clay, made into a snake
- A citrine

Timing

Tuesday

The Spell

1. Wind the snake so it is knotted. Say, *"Snake in the grass, this wrong cannot pass. Yet I shall let you go, so future happiness I may know."*
2. Rub the snake all over with the citrine, saying, *"I send you nothing that is bad, I let you go in peace, for me new fun to be had, and if you are kinder one day be, may you find new happiness, but not with me."*
3. Wash your citrine, then dry it. Put it in your purse or bag if you are going somewhere you will meet your ex or if you are going out with friends.
4. Untangle the clay snake. Set it free in long grass and go have fun.
5. Keep your head high and wear your coolest outfit.

As you carry your citrine, it will call that smart, fun, and loyal new boy/girlfriend fast. However, you may choose to enjoy some time being independent if you like!

EASE ANXIETY

You will need

- An amethyst crystal
- A small bowl of water, the one you keep on your crystal altar is fine.

Timing

A few days before an examination/test or whatever coming situation is making you anxious

The Spell

1. Holding the amethyst in your writing hand, plunge it nine times into the water, pulling it out each time.
2. Then say nine times, *"Amethyst take away all panic and fear, that my mind will be totally clear, successful and happy I will be, amethyst hold my worry instead of me."*
3. Hold the stone in your non-writing hand anytime you feel anxious or scared about the future. Wash it afterward in your bowl of water to take away the worry the amethyst is holding instead of you.
4. Change the water each time afterward.

On the morning of the exam/test, interview, or nerve-causing situation, dip the amethyst in the water. Rub the amethyst in the center of your brow, saying the words again.

Take the amethyst with you and touch it before beginning whatever you are worried about, saying the words in your mind.

GOOD FORTUNE

This spell will work beautifully at a crystal party for up to seven people, each choosing a color for which they will hold the crystal, light the candle, and say the words.

You will need

- Seven small candles in a semicircle in your crystal place: red, orange, yellow, green, blue, purple, and white (start with red; white will be at the other end)
- Your seven rainbow crystals set in front of their own color candle (if you don't have all seven colors, use a glass bead or glass nugget for ones you don't yet own)

Timing

Whenever you want to ask the angels and cosmos for something special. Iris is the name of the goddess of the rainbow.

The spell

1. Sit or stand facing the candles.
2. Pick up the red crystal and say, *"I take the power of red to make my wish come true (name your wish)."*
   Light the red candle, saying, *"Iris, goddess of the rainbow, this I ask of you."*
   Return the red crystal to its place in front of its candle.
3. Pick up the orange crystal, saying, *"I take the power of orange to make my wish come true (name it again)."*
   Light the orange candle, saying, *"Iris, goddess of the rainbow, this I ask of you."*
   Return the orange crystal to its place.

4. Pick up the yellow crystal, saying, *"I take in the power of yellow to make my wish come true (name it)."*
   Light the yellow candle and say, *"Iris, goddess of the rainbow, this I ask of you."*
   Return the yellow crystal to its place.
5. Pick up the green crystal, saying, *"I take in the power of green to make my wish come true (name it again)."*
   Light the green candle, saying, *"Iris, goddess of the rainbow, this I ask of you."*
   Return the green crystal to its place.
6. Pick up the blue crystal, saying, *"I take the power of blue to make my wish come true (name it)."*
   Light the blue candle, saying, *"Iris, goddess of the rainbow, this I ask of you."*
   Return the blue crystal to its place.
7. Hold the purple crystal, saying, *"I take the power of purple to make my wish come true (name it)."*
   Light the purple candle, saying, *"Iris, goddess of the rainbow, this I ask of you."*
   Return the purple crystal to its place.
8. Finally, pick up the white crystal, saying, *"I take the power of white to make my wish come true (name it)."*
   Light the white candle, saying, *"Iris, goddess of the rainbow, this I ask of you."*
   Return the white crystal to its place.
9. Leave the candles to burn out.

STOP BULLYING

Seven obsidian arrows are well worth buying for your crystal treasure chest. You can keep them in a circle on the floor around your bed if you are ever spooked (facing inward to protect you). Turn them outward in your crystal place around an important assignment or printout of an application to draw success.

You will need

- Your seven obsidian arrows (if you don't have arrows, use any dark pointed crystals, such as smoky quartz)
- A picture of yourself (if possible, small pictures from social media of the bullies or, if not, their names written on separate squares of paper in red pen)
- A pair of scissors

Timing

Tuesday, a day associated with strength, courage, and action, is the anti-bullying day

The Spell

1. Put the arrows facing inward in a circle around the picture of you.
2. Set the pictures/names of the bullies around the outside of the arrows in a circle.
3. Pick up each arrow in turn, counterclockwise, saying for each as you touch it, *"Arrows fly swift and swift return, let these bullies from me turn, away I say, away, away, let only kindness and harmony stay."*
   Return each arrow to its position.

4. Take each picture of the bullies or their name papers in turn and cut each one in half, saying, *"I harm not you, but cut away your power, you can no longer threaten me from this hour."*
5. Throw the cut pictures into the garbage; have a small trash can nearby. Leave the picture of yourself inside the arrows for a full day and night.

ANTI-ENVY

You will need

- A mirror propped against the wall on a flat surface, big enough to reflect your head and shoulders
- A brown candle in the center of and in front of the mirror
- Your banded agate (choose one with an eye in the center) or tiger's-eye in front of the candle and closer to you

Timing

As darkness falls

The Spell

1. Light the candle and stand behind it so you are reflected in the mirror (not too near and no trailing sleeves).
2. Hold the crystal between your open-cupped hands toward the mirror so it is reflected in the mirror, saying, *"(name jealous person), reflected away is your jealousy, your malice, and your spite. The crystal sends back your own envy, that is only right."*
3. Press the crystal against your psychic third eye in the center of your brow, saying three times, *"Three by three, sent back from me, three by three, returned is your envy."*
4. Leave the candle to burn out.

Carry the crystal in a little bag or purse to protect you when next you see the jealous person.

SEEKING TRAVEL

You will need

- A picture of where you would like to travel or take your vacation
- Your labradorite or smoky quartz on top of the picture
- A rose incense stick or cone in a deep holder to catch the ash to the right of the picture

Timing

Wednesday, the day of travel and adventure, or Thursday if long distance or long term

The Spell

1. Light the incense. Pass the crystal nine times through the incense smoke, being careful not to burn yourself. Say nine times, *"Winds of the north, east, south, and west, come to me, let me travel where I most would like to be."*
   Return the crystal to its place.
2. When the incense is burned and cool, take the ash outdoors. Release it, saying, *"Winds of the north, east, south, and west as you fly free, carry me to where I most want to be (name destination or vacation plan again)."*
3. Keep the crystal with any brochures or printouts of the desired trip in your crystal place.

CHARM BAG FOR SUCCESS

You will need

- A mirror in which you can see your head and shoulders
- In front the mirror, a blue bag or purse
- On top of the purse or bag place two lapis lazuli and three turquoise for success

Timing

The morning before the exam/interview/audition

The Spell

1. Place the crystals in the bag or purse.
2. Close the bag. Facing the mirror, toss the bag five times, higher and higher, saying, *"Mirror, mirror on the wall, I shall not fail, I shall not fall, I shall succeed in every way, mirror let your shine bring success today."*
3. Throw the bag a sixth time and say as you catch it, *"Success is mine, mirror like you shall I shine."*

Take the crystal bag with you.

A CHARM BAG FOR GOOD LUCK

In this spell I have added a few kitchen ingredients that are magickally lucky, but you don't have to use them. We are only counting the crystals as charm bag items, and seven is a very lucky number.

You will need

- Three small aventurine or amazonites and four small blue or orange goldstones

- A very small magnet
- A green purse or bag
- Seven almonds or any nuts

Timing

Sunday morning

The Spell

1. Shake the crystals in your closed hands, saying seven times, "Seven, lucky seven, let fortune on me shine, may good luck from now on always be mine."
2. Add them to the bag along with the nuts and the magnet. Then say, *"Draw to me, good luck that I may see, everything I wish for (name) come to me."*
3. Close the bag and say, *"May all I say, come my way."*
4. Name how most you want that luck to happen.

Keep your bag hidden in your bedroom. Touch it whenever you need extra luck.

BANISH UNFRIENDLY SPIRITS

I suggest you don't use spirit communication boards, such as Ouija, with friends or try to call up spirits at a sleepover. Sometimes mischievous low-level spirits can come and try to first impress and then scare you. But, especially in old houses, you can get noisy spirits who are scary.

You will need

- Three purple candles and, to the right of them, two white ones
- Three amethysts, one in front of each purple candle, and two clear quartz (one in front of each white candle)

Timing

After dark

The Spell

1. Light the left-hand purple candle. Say, *"Be gone all specters of evil with the shining of this light. Ended is your power to terrify me, I call on the powers of light."*
2. Light the middle and then the right-hand purple candles, saying the same words for each candle.
3. Light the white candles in turn from the right-hand purple one.
4. Then extinguish each purple candle left to right one after the other. Don't blow the purple candles out, as blowing out a candle spreads energies. Instead snuff out the purple flames with a candlesnuffer, an old cup over the flame, or the back of a spoon (be careful you don't burn yourself).
5. Say, *"May all that is not good be extinguished with this light, to trouble me no more by day and night."*

6. Leave the white candles for a few minutes, then blow them out, saying, *"Surround me with the light."*
7. Put an amethyst crystal at the 3, 6, and 9 o'clock positions on the sun cross shown below and a clear quartz at 12 o'clock. Set the other quartz in the center.

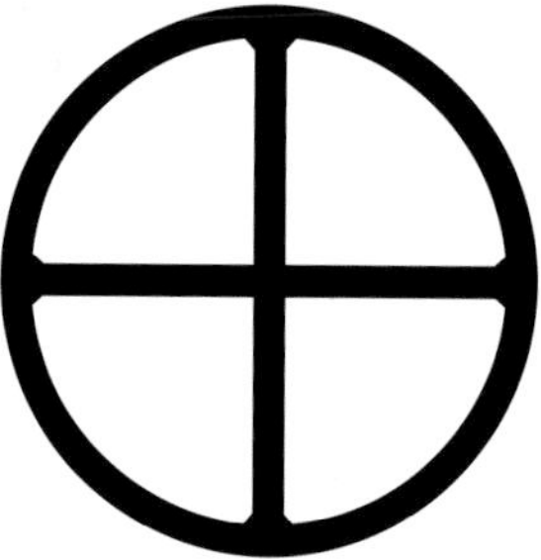

Keep this layout on your bedside table or in your crystal place to drive away all spooks.

APPENDIX B:
BONUS CRYSTALS AND THEIR MEANING

Amber

Orange fossilized tree resin.

• confidence • takes away obstacles we put in our own way by feeling we aren't good enough to succeed • helps if you are shy or hate parties • for happy families • fixing a relationship after problems • attracts love and money since it is slightly magnetic • brings memories of past lives • connects with fairies and nature spirits • feeling attractive as you are if you are being teased • calming if you have eating problems

Aquamarine

Pale blue or bluish green, see-through.

• for travel, especially overseas • protects against accidents • calms angry or bad-tempered people and panic attacks • helps if you are pressured to achieve impossible standard • soothes travel sickness • good if neighbors or teachers are always complaining about you to parents • brings love • connects you with water spirits • healing

Calcite

Pale orange, sometimes looks like ice.

• encourages you to start again if you have failed an exam or been let down in love • calms hormones • heals hurts and abuse from the past • for fun evenings with friends, family, or boy/girlfriend • eases tensions in family or stepfamilies • healing

Calcite, blue

Pale to medium blue, sometimes looks like ice.

• cools and calms you when you or someone close is angry • relaxes you if you are always trying to do a hundred things at once • to be taken seriously if no one listens to you • good for sensitive pets • connects with air and water spirits • for safety and success in water sports • keeps your smartphone, tablet, computer, and other precious things safe • helps memory for tests, interviews, and examinations • offers focus for study if it is hard to concentrate • healing

Calcite, green

Pale to medium green, sometimes looks like ice.

• reduces hyperactivity or bad habits that spoil your everyday life • helps to make friends if you are shy • protective if you spend a lot of time on your technology • guards against attacks on social media • for backpacking and camping • attracts money through new chances to earn it • calls earth spirits • for healthy eating • overcomes food issues and phobias • healing

Celestine, orange

Medium to bright orange, unpolished, looks like ice crystals with holes

• confidence to follow your own ideas • for reassuring pets who are alone in the day • independence • helps you settle in a new school, job, or home • for resolving eating problems and feeling good about yourself • brings out psychic gifts and helps you to trust your intuition • healing

Howlite, white

Bright white with gray or black veins, the undyed form of blue howlite.

• for healing and health • sticking to study and homework • a natural stress defuser • encourages pets, especially cats, not to stray • brings success in art or music • overcomes fear of dark • encourages you to take care of details if you always want to finish fast • healing

Kunzite

Lilac or pink with lines down it.

• the driver's crystal, whether you drive your own vehicle or are learning to drive • guards against other drivers' aggressiveness • keeps you calm in heavy traffic • calms exam nerves • good for younger women harmonizing with hormonal swings and menstrual cycles • lifts depression • communicating with angels and spirit guardians • drives away spooks and nasty spirits • helps sleep and peaceful dreams if you spend a lot of time working with technology or on social media late in the evening • healing

Lodalite

Clear with mixed color inclusions; brown tendrils inside, making scenes of forests or magick landscapes; called the Dream Crystal, it is expensive but well worth saving for or asking for one as a special-occasion gift.

• for beautiful and magickal past life dreams • good for travel in sleep while knowing you are dreaming • increases psychic powers • for contacting nature spirits and connection with wildlife • for absent healing and for skin problems

APPENDIX C:

A TREASURY OF CRYSTALS

This section lists common issues and which crystals apply. You can then check back in the references in Appendix B or in the index to read more about a specific crystal.

Allergies:

• adventurine • clear quartz • lemon chrysophase • clear quartz • citrine • jade

Angels/guardian spirits:

• angelite • blue celestine • blue howlite • pink and lilac kunzite • blue lace agate • opalite • rose quartz • rutilated quartz • selenite

Anxiety:

• amethyst • citrine • adventurine • jade

Brilliant ideas, creativity, auditions, and performances:

• aventurine • chrysocolla • clear quartz • all goldstones • lapis lazuli • rutilated quartz • sunstone • red and golden tiger's-eye

Depression:

• banded agate • smoky quartz

Dreams, knowing you are dreaming, traveling in dreams:

• amethyst • blue howlite • lodalite • opalite • rutilated quartz • selenite • smoky quartz

Fairies, nature spirits:

Amber • aquamarine • blue calcite • dendritic agate • jade • lodalite • opalite • rutilated quartz

Fame and fortune:

• chrysocolla • clear quartz • all goldstones • sunstone • tiger's-eye • turquoise

Fears of flying and travel, safety for long-distance travel and backpacking overseas:

• aquamarine • blue celestine • malachite • moonstone • selenite • sodalite • turquoise

Fears, phobias, and cravings:

• amethyst • aquamarine • any calcite • any fluorite • black onyx • rose quartz • smoky quartz • sodalite

Food problems and weight/image issues:

• amber • mangano or pink calcite • orange calcite • carnelian • orange celestine • moonstone • rose quartz

Fortune-telling:

• amethyst • aventurine • carnelian • citrine • clear quartz • hematite • red jasper • lapis lazuli • moonstone • black onyx • rose quartz • smoky quartz • sodalite • golden tiger's-eye • turquoise

Friends, popularity, feeling attractive:

• amber • aventurine • carnelian • clear quartz • dendritic agate • orange goldstone • rose quartz • sunstone • turquoise

Ghosts and Spirits:

• amethyst • clear quartz • purple fluorite • pink and lilac kunzite • moonstone • obsidian arrows • smoky quartz • sodalite • golden tiger's-eye

Good luck:

• amazonite • aventurine • green chrysoprase • all goldstones • selenite • smoky quartz (also reverses bad luck) • sunstone

Happiness, celebrations, family togetherness:

• amber • banded agate • orange calcite • carnelian • citrine • dendritic agate • blue lace agate • opalite • rose quartz • selenite • sunstone • turquoise

Headaches:

• amethyst • purple flourite

Healing and health:

• amethyst • aquamarine • all calcites • carnelian • clear quartz • citrine • white howlite • red jasper • rose quartz • smoky quartz • sunstone

Hormones, PMS, problems with body changes, and menstrual issues:

• aquamarine • bloodstone • mangano calcite • orange calcite • carnelian • white howlite • red jasper • pink and lilac kunzite • moonstone • rose quartz • selenite

Independence/leadership:

• amazonite • carnelian • orange celestine • chrysocolla • all goldstones • sunstone • turquoise

Love:

• amber • aquamarine • aventurine • green chrysoprase • hematite • jade • moonstone • rose quartz • selenite • sunstone

Money-making:

• amber • aventurine • green calcite • citrine • dendritic agate • blue or orange goldstone • hematite • jade • sunstone • golden-brown and red tiger's-eye

Nightmares:

• amethyst • moonstone • opalite • selenite • rose quartz • smoky quartz

Past lives, awake and in dreams:

• amethyst • blue celestine • purple fluorite • blue howlite • lodalite • moonstone • opalite • selenite • smoky quart

Protection against accidents, falls and injuries, and damage to property:

• aquamarine • aventurine • blue calcite • carnelian • smoky quartz • turquoise

Protection for animals:

• any banded agate • orange celestine • jade • blue and green calcite • purple fluorite • obsidian • turquoise •

Protection against bullying and physical danger:

bloodstone • blue and orange celestine • chrysocolla • red jasper • black obsidian arrows • red tiger's-eye

Protection against jealousy, spite, and liars, and against emotional vampires who drain your energy:

• any banded agate with an eye in the center • chrysocolla • citrine • hematite • yellow jasper • moonstone • obsidian arrows • smoky quartz • sugilite • tiger's-eye in all colors • black tourmaline • turquoise

Protection against social media attacks:

• green calcite • chrysocolla • malachite • obsidian arrows • black onyx • smoky quartz • black tourmaline

Psychic powers:

• amethyst • blue and orange celestine • green chrysoprase • clear quartz • crystal balls, pyramids, and pendulums • purple fluorite • lodalite • rutilated quartz • smoky quartz • sugilite

Spirit Guardians and Nature Spirits:

• dendritic agate • blue howlite • jade • lodalite • rutilated quartz • turquoise

Strength and Stamina:

• clear quartz • red jasper • red tiger's-eye

Stress:

• blue lace agate • lapiz lazuli • mangano calcite • rose quartz • clear quartz • orange calcite • carnelian

Shyness, fear of speaking in public, going to new places, staying away from home:

• carnelian • blue and orange celestine • orange goldstone • blue lace agate • sugilite • turquoise

Skin problems, worries about appearance:

• angelite • mangano or pink calcite • carnelian • blue lace agate • lodalite • rose quartz

Sleeplessness:

• amethyst • blue celestine • purple fluorite • moonstone • rose quartz • selenite • sodalite

Sports and fitness:

• bloodstone • blue calcite • red jasper • sunstone • red tiger's-eye

Study, learning, concentration, interviews, exams and tests, including driving tests:

• blue calcite • citrine • purple fluorite • white howlite • yellow jasper • lapis lazuli • blue lace agate • black onyx • rutilated quartz • black tourmaline turquoise

Travel:

• aquamarine • green calcite • blue or orange celestine • citrine • dendritic agate • kunzite • moonstone • sodalite • turquoise

APPENDIX D: MAGICKAL FRAGRANCES

MAGICKAL HERBS

Use herbs in teas, strained to sprinkle around crystals or precious items; as smudge sticks or incense; or as sprigs of fresh herbs or dried herbs from the supermarket spice section. Add dried herbs to your crystal charm bags.

Match the meaning of the magickal herbs with the meaning of the crystals you are using.

Allspice

• unexpected or fast money • anything urgent • fun and parties • moving along anything that is stuck or just not happening

Basil

• going steady • a special love • loyalty in friends • protection against aggressive people and animals • conquers fear of flying • saving money for something important

Cedar/cedarwood

• removing bad habits and negative thoughts • harmony and happiness • working toward big ambitions • healing • clearing away bad energies from your room • transport or possessions

Chamomile

• happiness • making people kinder • caring for children and animals • reverses bad luck • a slow increase in funds • happy family matters and celebrations • healing

Cinnamon (be careful as this can burn if you get it too near your eyes or mouth)

speedy good results in whatever you want • being asked out by someone you really like • regaining money after loss • psychic powers • for an exciting trip

Dragon's blood

• fierce protection against bullies • guards against those who say or think nasty things about you • anti-spook • for success in any major project or assignment, physical fitness, and competitive sports • healing

Fennel

• travel • new opportunities in study or training • independence • swift good results in anything new • keeps harm away from people, animals, and places

Frankincense

• fame and fortune • successful auditions and chances to shine • leadership • courage • joy • long-term career plans • success • overseas or interstate travel • good in spells and when you are doing readings

Hyssop

• a faithful love • psychic powers • spirituality • all forms of protection, especially from paranormal attack and envy • sprinkle the liquid from hyssop tea (use tea bags and hot water) around anything that feels unlucky • healing • getting a place on a team or in a prestigious club

Juniper

• clears the home after quarrels, sickness, and bad luck • protects against accidents and having your precious things stolen • a new start wherever you want or need it

Lemongrass/lemon

• drives away spite, lies, gossip, and human snakes, on- and offline • psychic powers • travel • study • getting homework finished quickly and obtaining good marks

Lemon verbena

• breaking a run of bad luck • protection against envy, anger, and people who wish you harm • feeling attractive if you are teased about your appearance or worry about your image

Mint and peppermint

• for getting noticed in a good way • for memorizing facts and organizing your life and study • drives bad vibes from the home • brings chances to earn more money • health • travel • new love

Myrrh

• mending quarrels • getting over grief after the loss of an elderly relative or a beloved pet • protection against danger of all kinds, on- and offline • for crystal spells, especially moon magick and crystal readings • for healing

Pine

• drives away harm to home and family • makes you awake and alert if you're feeling tired and out of sorts • for the success of any creative venture • for new beginnings • for sorting out your room • for privacy if brothers and sisters invade your space and tell tales about you

Rosemary

• for love and visions or dreams of future love • drives away malevolence from the paranormal world • protection from threats by people who claim to call up spirits • for learning, study, and a good memory • foretelling the future

Sage

• for long-term plans and learning • growing health • success in examinations, interviews, tests, and presentations • talent contests and leadership bids • a good memory and ability to concentrate on studies • saving for something special

Sandalwood

• for leadership • opportunities to stand out from the crowd • for prizes, awards, and rewards • for getting more money • truth coming out if you have been blamed unfairly • powerful in crystal readings and spells • healing

Tarragon

• called the dragon herb • for courage • protects against bullying on- and offline • unexpected help to solve old problems • speaking out over what matters to you and being heard • making a big step forward to fulfilling an ambition

Thyme

• dried thyme in a bag or scattered in circles around what needs protecting, guards your room and your precious items • health • memory of past lives • drives away nightmares and phantoms of the night • good for study and learning a lot of facts

Vetiver

• for love • healing • brings good luck after a run of bad luck • protects against spooks and scary experiences if you've called up spirits • stops people stealing your ideas or trying to come between you and friends

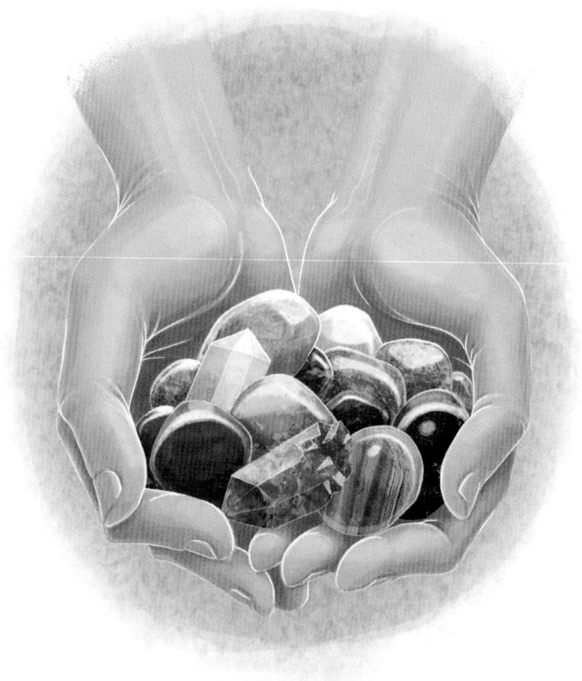

MAGICKAL FLOWERS

Use fragrant flowers as scented candles, incense, fragrant oils, perfume, cologne, or potpourri. Scatter petals, fresh or dried, around crystals. Match the crystal and floral meaning to double the power. You can also set a vase or pot of fragrant flowers in your crystal place to fill the crystals on your altar with what you most want and need.

Geranium

• for healing arguments and bad feelings at home, school, or the workplace • for first or new love • for romance • for money coming to you as a gift or as a prize or reward

Hyacinth

• for believing in yourself even if others make you doubt • to protect against cliques • for happy family and celebrations at home • rebuilding trust after betrayal • increasing radiance and charisma • attracting beautiful things and good friends into your life

Jasmine

• for romance • overcoming image problems or food issues • optimism about the future • changing your luck for the better • keeping and discovering secrets • for psychic powers • for magick spells, especially on the full moon, and crystal readings

Lavender

• love and romance • loving yourself and valuing yourself as you are rather than wishing you were different • happiness • health • travel • guards against cruelty and spite • reduces stress, fears, and phobias • for all healing rituals

Marigold

• increases happy energies in a room or building • protective against nightmares • if you have been accused unfairly or have had problems with authority figures • the happy growth of love and friendship

Rose

• an all-purpose fragrance • for love • mending quarrels • for growing confidence if you are shy • for all hormonal imbalances • for animals, especially young ones and nursing mothers • for any activities with children • for overcoming abuse or ill treatment • attracting money • all healing rituals

AFTERWORD

The most important fact to recall about crystals, whether you are working with your basic crystals or you are building up a special collection, is that crystals are millions of years old and are therefore very wise. Trust them to guide you as to which crystal is right for you and let it tell you what you need to know.

Love your crystals, polish them, listen to their soft voices in your mind, let them fill you with joy and happiness. When you are at the shore, in a forest clearing, or on a hillside or even the local park, look for the glint of crystal inside what may seem an ordinary stone.

Buy unpolished pieces of crystal still in their rock, for they are as precious as the finest jewel.

In this book I have taught you all you need to know to use crystals in your life and to hold special crystal parties with friends.

For now, light a candle. Without looking, choose a crystal from your collection. Hold it, make a wish, and let it guide you in your dreams to happiness and in your waking hours to reaching out for everything your heart desires.

My love,

Cassandra Eason, June 2019

INDEX

NOTE: Page numbers in **bold** indicate summaries of properties/uses of crystals. Page numbers in parentheses indicate intermittent references.

✳ NOTES ✳